Global Marketing Management

GLOBAL MARKETING MANAGEMENT

A. Pandu
Lecturer in Commerce
Indo-American College, Cheyyar-604 407
Thiruvannamalai District, Tamil Nadu.

GRP

GLOBAL RESEARCH PUBLICATIONS
NEW DELHI (INDIA)

First Published -*June 2008*

ISBN: 81-89630-10-5

Published by

GLOBAL RESEARCH PUBLICATIONS
4800/24, 1st Floor, Ansari Road
Darya Ganj, New Delhi-110002 (India)
Phone : 23245225. Fax : 91-11-23272135
E-mail: serials@satyam.net.in

DEDICATED TO

MY PARENTS

A. Pandu

Contents

PREFACE

First Edition of Global Marketing is invaluable text for M.Com., and MBA students studying international or Global Marketing. This book discusses the theory, dimensions, strategies and practice of global marketing against a back ground of liberalization, globalization, multilateral and regional economic integration. It is indispensable reference tool for business executives and marketing practitioners as well, as it covers topics from fundamental concept to the contemporary opportunities and challences of marketing.

A. PANDU
Lecturer in Commerce
Indo–American College, Cheyyar–604 407
Tamil Nadu

ACKNOWLEDGEMENT

The first edition of this book bears the impression of many people. My professors, students, colleagues, and associates continue to have an important impact in my thinking to write this book. Hence I am very much thankful to all of them for their generous support extended in completing the same.

In preparing this book I want to give special acknowledgement to Dr. Mohammed Gallib Hussain, HOD of Corporate Secretaryship and Research Supervisor, Islamiah College and Dr. S. Liyahath John, Professor of Economics, Islamiah College, Vaniyambadi, Dr. A. Krishnan, Professor of commerce in Govt. Arts and Science College, Dharmapuri, S. Kesavan, Professor of Commerce working in Government Arts College, Thiruthani, for their great influence, constructive criticism and tireless moral support in preparing this book.

I also want to acknowledge S. Karthikeyan and A. Ajaykumar for the fine and creative designs carried out in preparing this work.

I am very much thankful to my family members for their support extended in writing this book.

It is an honour for me to I thank almighty for giving me an opportunity and keeping me active in preparing this book.

A. PANDU

Lecturer in Commerce

Indo–American College, Cheyyar–604 407

Tamil Nadu

1 Introduction to Global Marketing

Introduction

Terms such as "global village" and "world economy" have become very fashionable. Marketing goods and services on a global scale can happen in an "engineered" way, but often it is as a result of good and meticulous planning. For example, in order to starve off potential famine, the United Nation's World Food Programme (WFP) may purchase maize from Zimbabwe and distribute it in Tanzania, Malawi and Kenya. This "engineered" international marketing.

The world is becoming increasingly interdependent for its economic progress. In 1954, in the USA, for instance, imports were only one percent of GNP, but in 1984 they had risen to 10%. In food crops, while developing countries trade in coffee, cocoa, cotton and sugar actually declined in value during the 1980s, developing countries as a group experienced annual export growth rates of 4 to 11% in categories like processed fruit and vegetables, fresh processed fish products, feed stuffs and oil seeds. High value food product exports in 1990 totaled approximately $144 billion, the same as crude petroleum, representing 5% of world commodity trade. In 1990, more than twenty Less Developed Countries (LDCs) had exports of high value foods exceeding $500 million including countries like Brazil, China, Thailand, India and Senegal which is indicated by the world development report made by World Bank.

The Evolution of Global Marketing

Whether an organization markets its goods and services domestically or internationally, the definition of marketing still applies. However, the scope of marketing is broadened when the organization decides to sell across international boundaries, this being primarily due to the numerous other dimensions which the organization has to account for. For example, the organization's language of business may be "English", but it may have to do business in the "French language". This not only requires a translation facility, but the French cultural conditions have to be accounted for as well. Doing business "the French way" may be different from doing it "the English way". This is particularly true when doing business with the Japanese.

Let us, firstly define "Marketing" and then see how, by doing marketing across multinational boundaries, differences, where existing, have to be accounted for.

S. Carter defines marketing as: "The process of building lasting relationships through planning, executing and controlling the conception, pricing, promotion and distribution of ideas, goods and services to create mutual exchange that satisfy individual and organizational needs and objectives".

The long held tenants of marketing are "customer value", "competitive advantage" and "focus". This means that organizations have to study the market, develop products or services that satisfy customer needs and wants, develop the "correct" marketing mix and satisfy its own objectives as well as giving customer satisfaction on a continuing basis. However, it became clear in the 1980s that this definition of marketing was too narrow. Preoccupation with the tactical workings of the marketing mix led to neglect of long term product development, so "Strategic Marketing" was born. The focus was shifted from knowing everything about the customer, to knowing the customer in a context which includes the competition, government policy and regulations, and the broader economic, social and political macro forces that shape the evolution of markets. In global marketing terms this means forging alliances (relationships) or developing networks, working closely with home country government officials and industry competitors to gain access to a target market. Also the marketing objective has changed from one of satisfying organizational objectives to one of "stakeholder" benefits-including employees, society, and government and so on. Profit is still essential but not an end in itself.

Strategic marketing according to Wensley (1982) has been defined as:

"Initiating, negotiating and managing acceptable exchange relationships with key interest groups or constituencies, in the pursuit of sustainable competitive advantage within specific markets, on the basis of long run consumer, channel and other stakeholder franchise".

Whether one takes the definition of "marketing" or "strategic marketing", "marketing" must still be regarded as both a philosophy and a set of functional activities. As a philosophy embracing customer value (or satisfaction), planning and organizing activities to meet individual and organizational objectives, marketing must be internalized by all members of an organization, because without satisfied customers the organization will eventually die. As a set of operational activities, marketing embraces selling, advertising, transporting, market research and product development activities to name but a few. It is important to note that marketing is not just a philosophy or one or some of the operational activities. It is both. In planning for marketing, the organization has to basically decide what it is going to sell, to which target market and with what marketing mix (product, place, promotion, price and people). Although these tenants of marketing planning must apply anywhere, when marketing across national boundaries, the difference between domestic and international marketing lies almost entirely in the differences in national environments within which the global programme is conducted and the differences in the organization and programmes of a firm operating simultaneously in different national markets.

It is recognized that in the "postmodern" era of marketing, even the assumptions and long standing tenants of marketing like the concepts of "consumer needs", "consumer sovereignty", "target markets" and "product/market processes" are being challenged. The emphasis is towards the emergence of the "customizing consumer", that is, the customer who takes elements of the market offerings and moulds a customized consumption experience out of these. Even further, post modernism, posts that the consumer who is the consumed, the ultimate marketable image, is also becoming liberated from the sole role of a consumer and is becoming a producer. This reveals itself in the desire for the consumer to become part of the marketing process and to experience immersion into "thematic settings" rather than merely to encounter products. So in consuming food products for example, it becomes not just a case of satisfying hunger needs, but also can be rendered as an image - producing act. In the post modern market place the product does not project images, it fills images. This is true in some foodstuffs. The consumption of "designer water" or "slimming foods" is a statement of a self image, not just a product consuming act.

Acceptance of postmodern marketing affects discussions of products, pricing, advertising, distribution and planning. However, given the fact that this textbook is primarily written with developing economies in mind, where the environmental conditions, consumer sophistication and systems are not such that allow a quantum leap to postmodernism, it is intended to mention the concept in passing. Further discussion on the topic is available in the accompanying list of readings. When organizations develop into global marketing organizations, they usually evolve into this from a relatively small export base. Some firms never get any further than the exporting stage. Marketing overseas can, therefore, be anywhere on a continuum of "foreign" to "global". It is well to note at this stage that the words "international", "multinational" or "global" are now rather outdated descriptions. In fact "global" has replaced the other terms to all intents and purposes. "Foreign" marketing means marketing in an environment different from the home base, it's basic form being "exporting". Over time, this may evolve into an operating market rather than a foreign market. One such example is the Preferential Trade Area (PTA) in Eastern and Southern Africa where involved countries can trade inter-regionally under certain common modalities. Another example is the Cold Storage Company of Zimbabwe.

The Four Stages of Global Marketing Evolution

1. *Stage One:* domestic in focus, with all activity concentrated in the home market. Whilst many organizations can survive like this, for example raw milk marketing, solely domestically oriented organizations are probably doomed to long term failure.
2. Stage *Two:* home focus, but with exports (ethnocentric). Probably believes only in home values, but creates an export division. Usually ripe for the taking by stage four organizations.
3. *Stage Three:* stage two organizations which realize that they must adapt their marketing mixes to overseas operations. The focus switches to multinational (polycentric) and adaption becomes paramount.
4. *Stage Four:* global organizations which create value by extending products and programmes and focus on serving emerging global markets (geocentric). This involves recognizing that markets around the world consist of similarities and differences and that it is possible to develop a global strategy based on similarities to obtain scale economies, but also recognizes and responds to cost effective differences. Its strategies are a combination of extension, adaptation and creation. It is unpredictable in behavior and always alert to opportunities.

There is no time limit on the evolution process. In some industries, like horticulture, the process can be very quick.

Factors which have led to Globalization

There have been many underlying forces, concepts and theories which have emerged as giving political explanation to the development of international trade. Remarkably, despite the

Stages of Domestic to Global Evolution

Management emphasis	*Stage one Domestic*	*Stage two International*	*Stage Three Multinational*	*Stage Four Global*
Focus	Domestic	Ethnocentric	Polycentric	Geocentric
Marketing strategy	Domestic	Extension	Adaption	Extension
Structure	Domestic	International	Worldwide	Adapation Creation Matrix/mixed
Management style	Domestic	Centralized top down	Decentralized bottom up	Integrated
Manufacturing	Mainly	Mainly	Host country	Lowest cost
Stance	Domestic	Domestic		world wide
Invest	Domestic	Domestic used	Mainly in each	Cross
Policy		world wide	host country	Subsidization
Performance evaluation	Domestic market share	Agaist home country market share	Each host country market share	World wide

trend to world interdependency, some countries have been less involved than others. The USA, for example, has a remarkably poor export record. About 2000 US companies only account for more than 70% of US manufacturer's exports. This has been mainly due to its huge statewide domestic market, which is almost tantamount to "international trade", for example, Californian fruit being sold three thousand kilometers away in New Jersey. Japan has risen fast to dominate the export rankings, with countries of Africa struggling to make a significant mark, mainly because of their emphasis on exporting primary products. This section will briefly examine the forces which have been instrumental in the development of world trade.

International Product Trade Cycle

From a high income country point of view phase 1 involves exporting, based on domestic product strength and surplus-to phase 2, when foreign production begins, to phase 3 when production in the foreign country becomes competitive, to phase 4 when import competition begins. The assumption behind this cycle is that new products are firstly launched in high income markets because (a) there is most potential and (b) the product can be tested best domestically near its source of production. Thus new products generally emanate from high income countries and, over time, orders begin to be solicited from lower income countries and so a thriving export market develops. High income country entrepreneurs quickly realize that the markets to which they are selling often have lower production costs and so production is initiated abroad for the new products, so starts the second stage.

In the second stage of the cycle, foreign and high income country production begins to supply the same export market. As foreign producers begin to expand and gain more experience, their competition displaces the high income export production source. At this point high income countries often decide to invest in foreign countries to protect their share. As foreign producers expand, their growing economies of scale make them a competitive source for third country markets where they compete with high income exporters. The final phase of the cycle occurs when the foreign producer achieves such a scale and experience that it starts exporting to the original high income producer at a production cost lower than its original high income producer at a production cost lower than its original high income supplier. High income producers, once enjoying a monopoly in their own market, now face competition at home.

The cycle continues as the production capability in the product extends from other advanced countries to less developed countries at home, then in international trade, and finally, in other advanced countries home markets.

Whilst the underlying assumption behind the International Product Trade Cycle is that the cycle begins with the export of new product ideas from high income countries to low income importers, and then low income countries begin production of the product etc., things do not always turn out as the cycle suggests. Sometimes a high or even low income exporter may put a product into a high/low income country which is simply unable to respond. In this case, the Trade Cycle ceases to be the underpinning concept. This may be due to a number of factors like lack of access to capital to build the facilities to respond to the import, lack of skills or that the costs of local production cannot get down to the level of costs of the imported product. In this case, product substitution between the exporter and importer may also take place. A classic example of this phenomenon is the case of Zimbabwe Suns plash fruit juice drinks.

Orientation of Management

Perlmutter[1] (1967) identified distinctive "orientations" of management of international organizations. His "EPRG" scheme identified four types of attitudes or orientations associated with successive stages in the evolution of international operations.

- Ethnocentrism-home country orientation- exporting surplus.
- Polycentrism-host country orientation-subsidiary operation.

- Regiocentrism-regional orientation-world market strategies.
- Geocentrism-world orientation-world market strategies.

The latter two are based on similarities and differences in markets, capitalizing on similarities to obtain cost benefits, but recognizing differences.

Market Forces and Development

Over the last few decades internationalism has grown because of a number of market factors which have been driving development forward, over and above those factors which have been attempting to restrain it. These include market and marketing related variables.

Many global opportunities have arisen because of the clustering of market opportunities worldwide. Organisations have found that similar basic segments exist worldwide and, therefore, can be met with a global orientation. Cotton, as an ingredient in shirting's, suiting's, and curtain material can be globally marketed as natural and fashionable. One can see in the streets of New York, London, Kuala Lumpar or Harare, youth with the same style and brand of basketball shirts or American Football shorts. Coca Cola can be universally advertised as "Adds Life" or appeal to a basic instinct " You can't beat the Feeling" or "Come alive" as with the case of Pepsi. One can question "what feeling?", but that is not the point. The more culturally unbounded the product is, the more a global clustering can take place and the more a standardized approach can be made in the design of marketing programmes.

This standardized approach can be aided and abetted with technology. Technology has been one of the single most powerful driving forces to internationalism. Rarely is technology culturally bound. A new pesticide is available almost globally to any agricultural organization as long as it has the means to buy it. Computers in agriculture and other applications are used universally with IBM and Macintosh becoming household names. The need to recoup large costs of research and development in new products may force organizations to look at global markets to recoup their investment. This is certainly true of many veterinary products. Global volumes allow continuing investment in R & D, thus helping firms to improve quality. Farm machinery, for example, requires volume to generate profits for the development of new products.

Communications and transport are shrinking the global market place. Value added manufacturers like Cadbury, Nestlè, Kelloggs, Beyer, Norsk Hydro, Massey Ferguson and ICI find themselves "under pressure" from the market place and distributors alike to position their brands globally. In many cases this may mean an adaption in advertising appeals or messages as well as packaging and instructions. Nestle will not be in a hurry to repeat its disastrous experience of the "Infant formula" saga, whereby it failed to realize that the ability t find, boiled water for its preparations, coupled with the literacy level to read the instructions properly, were not universal phenomenon.

Marketing globally also provides the marketer with five types of "leverage" or "advantages", those of experience, scale, resource utilization and global strategy. A multi-product global giant like Nestle', with over £ 10 billion turnover annually, operates in so many markets, buys so much raw material from a variety of out growers of different sizes, that its international leverage is huge. If it consumes a third of the world's cocoa output annually, then it is in a position to dominate terms. This also has its dangers.

The greatest lift to producers of raw agricultural products has been the almost universal necessity to consume their produce. If one considers the whole range of materials from their raw to value added state there is hardly a market segment which cannot be tapped globally. Take, for example, oranges. Not only are Brazilian, Israeli, South African and Spanish oranges in demand in their raw state worldwide, but their downstream developments are equally in demand. Orange juice, concentrates, segments and orange pigments are globally demanded. In addition the ancillary products and services required to make the orange industry work, find themselves equally in global demand. So insecticides, chemicals, machinery, transport services, financial institutions, warehousing, packaging and a whole range of other production and marketing services are in demand, many provided by global organizations like Beyer, British Airways and Barclays Bank. Of course, many raw materials are at the mercy of world prices, and so many developing countries find themselves at the mercy of supply and demand fluctuations. But this highlights one important global lesson-the need to study markets carefully. Tobacco producing countries of the world are finding this out. With a growing trend away from tobacco products in the west, new markets or increasing volumes into consuming markets have to be prospected and developed. Many agricultural commodities take time to mature. An orange grove will mature after five years. By that time another country may plant or have its trees mature. Unless these developments are picked up by global intelligence the plans for a big profit may be not realized as the extra volume supplied depresses prices. This happened in 1993/94 with the Malawian and Zimbabwean tobacco companies. The unexpected release of Chinese tobacco depressed the tobacco price well below expectations, leaving farms with stock and large interest carrying production loans.

A number of suppliers of agricultural produce can take advantage of "off season" in other countries, or the fact that they produce specialty products. This is the way by which many East African and South American producers established themselves in Europe and the USA respectively. In fact the case of Kenya vegetables to Europe is a classic, covering many of the factors which have just been discussed-improved technology, emerging global segments, shrinking communications gaps and the drive to diversify product ranges.

The International Economic System

Several factors have contributed to the growth of the international economy post World War II. The principal forces have been the development of economic blocs like the

European Union (EU) and then the "economic pillars"- the World Bank (or International Bank for Reconstruction and Development to give its full name), the International Monetary Fund (IMF) and the evolution of the World Trade Organization from the original General Agreement on Tariffs and Trade (GATT).

Until 1969 the world economy traded on a gold and foreign exchange base. This affected liquidity drastically. After 1969 liquidity was eased by the agreement that member nations to the IMF accept the Special Drawing Rights (SDR) in settling reserve transactions. Now an international reserve facility is available. Recently, the World Bank has taken a very active role in the reconstruction and development of developing country economies, a point which will be expanded on later.

Until the General Agreement on Tariffs and Trade (GATT) after World War II, the world trading system had been restricted by discriminating trade practices. GATT had the intention of producing a set of rules and principles to liberalize trade. The most favored nation concept (MFN), whereby each country agrees to extend to all countries the most favorable terms that it negotiates with any country, helped reduce barriers. The "round" of talks began with Kennedy in the 60s and Tokyo of the 70s. The latest round, Uruguay, was recently concluded in April 1994 and ratified by most countries in early 1995. Despite these trade agreements, non tariff barriers like exclusion deals, standards and administrative delays are more difficult to deal with. A similar system exists with the European Union-the Lomè convention. Under this deal, African and Caribbean countries enjoy favored status with EU member countries.

Relative global peace has endangered confidence in world trade. Encouraged by this and the availability of finance, global corporations have been able to expand into many market.The break up of the former Soviet Union has opened up vast opportunities to investors, aided by the World Bank and the European Development Bank.This atmosphere of peace has also allowed the steady upward trend of domestic growth and again opened up market opportunities domestically to foreign firms. Peace in Mozambique, the "normalization" of South Africa, and peace in Vietnam as examples have opened up the way for domestic growth and also, therefore, foreign investment. The liberation of economies under World Bank sponsored structural adjustment programmes has also given opportunities. This is very true of countries like Zambia and Zimbabwe, where in the latter, for example, over Z$2.8 billion of foreign investment in the stock exchange and mining projects have occurred in the early 1990s.

Sometimes, market opportunities open up through "Acts of God". The great drought of 1992 in Southern Africa necessitated a large influx of foreign produce, especially yellow maize from the USA and South America.

Not only did this give a market for maize only, but opened up opportunities for transport businesses and services to serve the drought stricken areas. Speedy communications like air transportation and electronic data transmission and technology have "shrunk" the world. Costs and time have reduced enormously and with the advent of television, people can see what is happening elsewhere and this can cause desire levels to rise dramatically. Only recently has television been introduced into Tanzania, for example, and this has brought the world and its markets, closer to the average Tanzanian.

No doubt a great impetus to global trade was brought about by the development of economic blocs, and, conversely, by the collapse of others. Blocs like the European Union (EU), ASEAN, the North American Free Trade Agreement (NAFTA) with the USA, Canada and Mexico has created market opportunities and challenges. New countries are trying to join these blocs all the time, because of the economic, social and other advantages they bring. Similarly, the collapse of the old communist blocs have given rise to opportunities for organizations as they strive to get into the new market based economies rising from the ruins. This is certainly the case with the former Soviet bloc.

In the late 1980s and early 90s, the United States, along with Japan, have been playing an increasingly influential role in world affairs, especially with the collapse of the former USSR. Whilst on the one hand this is good, as the USA is committed to world welfare development, it can be at a price. The Gulf War coalition of the 90s, primarily put together by the USA as the leading player, was an example of the price.

Impetus to Global Marketing Involvement

Individuals or organizations may get involved in International Marketing in a rather unplanned way which gives the impetus to more formal and larger operations. This may happen in a number of ways:

Foreign Customers

Unsolicited enquiries through word of mouth, visits, exhibitions, and experience through others may result in orders. This is often typical of small scale organizations.

Importers

Importers may be looking for products unavailable in domestic markets, for example, mangoes in the UK, or products which can be imported on more favorable terms. An example of these is flowers from Kenya to Holland.

Intermediaries

These may be of four types-domestic based export merchants, domestic based export agents, export management companies or cooperative organizations. These will be expanded on later in this text. Sometimes an intermediary may provide export services in an attempt to reduce their own costs on the export of their own produce by acting as a representative for other organizations. This is called "piggybacking".

Other Sources

These may include banks, export organizations like ZIMTRADE, parastatals like the Kenyan Horticultural Crop Development Authority or even individual executives.

Behavior as a Global Marketing Impetus

We saw earlier in the internationalization process that organizations may evolve from exporting surplus or serving ad hoc enquiries to a more committed global strategy. This gradual change may involve moving from geographically adjacent markets to another, say, for example from the Southern African Development Conference (SADC) to Europe. However, not all globalization takes place like this. In the case of fresh cut flowers, these may go to major, developed country consumer centres, for example from Harare to London or Amsterdam and Frankfurt. Lusaka or Nairobi may never see Zimbabwe flowers. In analyzing behaviour one has not to generalize. What is certain is that in all stages, the balance of opportunity and risk is considered.

The Context of Internationalization

It is essential to see in what context individual organizations view internationalization. The existing situation of the firm will affect its interest in and ability to internationalize. Such may be the low domestic quality and organization that a firm could never export. It may not have the resources or the will.

Internationalization Infrastructure

Johanson and Mattison[5] (1984) have explored the notion of differences in tasks facing organizations which internationalize. In low and high infrastructure situations. "Early starters" are likely to experiment or depend on contacts with experienced organizations which know the process. "Late starters" may use existing contacts as a "bridge" to new opportunities. They may also be pressurized by customers, supplies or competitors to get into joint venturing. Joint venturing, with its added infrastructure, may lead to rapid progress. If the organization faces intense competition then it may be forced to up the pace and scale of foreign investment. Rising protectionism in recent years has given impetus to late starters to establish production facilities in target markets. Infrastructure for foreign operations may also change (firms also reduce their investment as well as invest). When this happens the perceived risk changes also.

This discussion on international infrastructure concludes the factors which have led to internationalization. It is a complex focus of internal and external factors and looking carefully at risk versus opportunities.

Planning to Meet the Opportunities and Challenges of Global Marketing

In order to take advantage of global opportunities, as well as meet the challenges presented by so doing a number of concepts can be particularly useful. Every organization needs an understanding of what is involved in "strategy", or else the haphazardness involved in chance exporting can be accepted as the norm with all inherent dangers involved. Also potential exporters need to know what is going on in the global "environment". Just as in domestic marketing "Government" "competition", "social" and other factors need to be accounted for; such is the case in international marketing. If one can place products or services at a point on an environmental sensitivity/ insensitivity continuum, one can see more clearly the need to account for differences in the marketing mix. By comparing the similarities and differences between domestic and international marketing needs and planning requirements, then the organization is in a better position to isolate the key factors critical to success. This section examines all these concepts in brief.

Strategy

Whatever business we are in, haphazard organization often leads to haphazard results. In planning for international marketing organizations need a clear picture of the steps involved. "Strategy" gives such a picture. Strategy is the response of the organization to the realities of shareholders and the business environment. The phases in the strategy formulation process are as follows.

The Global Environment

Of all the steps in formulating strategy, no one step is as important as the ability to assess the "environmental" factors in international marketing. Taking account of cultural, economic and political differences is a must when dealing with different markets. More will be said on these factors in later chapters. Environmental analysis allows the organization to cluster markets according to similarities and differences, based on the environmental "uncontrollable" factors. The international "uncontrollable" are in addition to the organization's domestic "uncontrollable" so need to be treated with extra care. Figure 1.4 shows the major environmental factors to be considered. It must be noted that according to the "relationship" marketing school of thought, the so called "incontrollable" can be made more "controllable" by building relationships with the influences of these factors. For example, if an exporter of horticultural produce wishes to be able to anticipate changes in the political environment, it may build a relationship with certain politicians who may have intimate knowledge of the political system. This should not, of course, be misconstrued as "insider information". However, having made this caveat, this text will treat the "incontrollable" in the conventional way.

Foreign "Uncontrollable"-in the Global Macro Environment

International Environment

An analysis of the environmental uncontrollable allows the potential marketers to place products on a continuum of environmental sensitivity. At the one end are environmentally insensitive products and at the other end, those more sensitive to economic, socio cultural, physical and other factors. The greater the sensitivity, the greater the need for the organization to learn the way the product interacts with the environment.

Framework for International Analysis

In order to put together the task of finding the differences and similarities in environmental and market analysis, a framework needs to be devised. Where unifying influences are found then the marketer is able to develop more standardized plans. When there are a large number of differences, then plans have to be designed adapted to circumstances a framework for the process of identifying similarities and differences.

A Conceptual Framework for Multinational Marketing: National Market versus other Nations

Once having identified the unifying and differentiating influences and answered many questions about where one could or could not standardize the marketing planning process then a conceptual framework for multinational marketing planning can be developed. One such conceptual framework is given below.

Conceptual Framework for Multinational Marketing in Constraint Economies

Key questions for analysis, planning and control of marketing in constraint economies.

(a) Principle Constraint Analysis

(i) Government's attitude to employment, foreign intervention, foreign exchange, indebtedness and policies.

(ii) Government's policy of economic development, foreign exchange, barter deals, equity arrangements, remittance of funds, state intervention, private sector development and import substitution?

(iii) Government's social objectives including indigenization, subsidies, population and socialization?

(iv) Laws, tariffs, duties, trade regulations, balance of payments, licensing and labour laws?

⇓

Leading to an economic analysis

⇓

Gathering *of appropriate* data on:

(b) Appropriate Environmental Variable Data

(i) Market characteristics-physical, cultural, size, growth rate, stage of development?

(ii) Market institutions-distribution, media, research, services?

(iii) Industry conditions-size, practices, development stage, appropriate technology?

(iv) Resources-manpower and money?

Planning

(c) Target country experts or generalist staff to plan operations?

(d) What are the *authorized* target markets and the product appropriateness? .

(e) Market size?

(f) What is the stage of development and strength of competition both state and private?

(g) What is the appropriate product/market technology?

(h) What is the necessary adaptation of the marketing mix?

(i) How do the government and company objectives coincide?

(j) What is the trading risk?

(k) What government/organization interface is required? How are licencies agreed and obtained? Who are the principle characters?

Structure

(l) How does the company have to be structured to meet the government, economic and social objectives as well as company objectives?

Plan Implementation

(m) Given the government's policies, attitudes and economic and social objectives how is an effective marketing plan designed, resourced and implemented? What degree of adaptation and cooperation is required at all levels? (Government marketing institutions and function)? Who will be responsible for each level"?

Controlling the Market Program

(n) Who is responsible and how is the plan performance measured and monitored?

(o) What controls, other than profit are required? Are employment and other such objectives necessary?

(p) Has the company the ability and authority to alter the parameters to bring actual results into line with desired?

(q) What are the principal control parameters? Can they be easily adjusted at all?

This framework is particularly relevant to developing economies where government constraints and controls tend to be more intensive than developed economies.

Product Life/Market Life Cycle

Just as in domestic marketing the concept of the Product Life Cycle has often been cited as a useful (but often maligned!) planning concept, so it can be useful in international marketing. An outline of the Market Life Cycle across international boundaries is give below.

The traditional four stage life cycle-introduction, growth, maturity, decline-is a well documented phenomenon. Attempts are made in the maturity stage to extend the cycle. The market life cycle is very similar and what global marketers have to be wary of is that not all markets are at the same stage globally. It may be appropriate to have tractor mounted ditchers and diggers in Africa or the UK where labour is not too plentiful, but in India, they may be the last thing required where labour is plentiful and very cheap. So the appropriate marketing strategy will be different for each market.

It would be very easy to discuss the global marketing decision as a case of deciding whether to export or standardize or adapt your product/ market offering. This is far from the caseEven the smallest nuance of change in the global environment can ruin a campaign or plan. Whilst the above discussion has tended to be theoretical in nature, most of it, if not all of it, is essential in practice. In food marketing systems many transactions and discussions take place across international boundaries. This involves a close look at all the necessary environmental factors. If one considers food marketing as the physical and economic bridge linking raw materials production and consumer purchases then a whole series of interdependent decisions, institutions, resource flows and physical and business activities take place. Food marketing stimulates and supports raw material production, balances commodity supply and demand and stimulates end demand and enhances consumer welfare. This process often transcends several different industries and markets, many of them crossing international boundaries. The product may change form, be graded, packed, transported and necessitate information flows, financial resources, invoice and retailing or wholesaling functions. In addition, quality standards designed for producers and transporters may apply as may product improvements. In other words, the bridge may involve a whole set of utilities afforded to the end user (time, place and form), and add value at each stage of the transaction. This system involves numerous independent and interdependent players and activities. To shift a perishable like strawberries 7000km from Harare, Zimbabwe to the UK requires an extraordinary complex series of activities, involving perfect timing. The detail involved in this intricate transaction will be explained in later chapters.

With commodities, physical, Government and economic environmental factors playing a major role in international marketing. So does price and quality differentiation. In later years the enormous success of the Brazilian frozen concentrated orange juice industry has been attributable not only to poor climatic conditions prevailing in its competitive countries, but the fact that its investment in large production economies of scale, bulk transport and storage technologies considerably reduced international transport costs and facilitated improved distribution of the juice to, and within, importing countries. From a cottage industry in 1970, it grew to account for 80% of world trade by the early 1990's. Its success, therefore, has been based on price and added value quality differentiation.

International marketing is, therefore, quite a complex operation, involving both an understanding of the theoretical and practical aspects involved. Prescriptions are totally inappropriate.

This concludes the discussion on the reasoning why internationalism has grown and the next chapters' took more closely at the environmental factors which have to be taken into account when considering to market internationally.

Objectives of Global Marketing

The following aims are sought to be achieved by studying marketing.

1. To develop an intelligent appreciation of modern marketing practices.
2. To provide guiding policies regarding marketing and their implement action.
3. To Study marketing problem according circumstance and to suggest solutions.
4. For analyzing short comings in the existing pattern of marketing.
5. To enable successful distribution of agricultural products, our mineral wealth and manufactured goods.
6. To enable the manager to assess and decide a particular course of action.
7. To revive existing marketing function if short comings are found to take appropriate actions in the course of action.

To find sources for further information concerning the market problem

Importance of Global Marketing

1. National income is composed of goods and service which money can buy.
2. Any increases in the efficiency of marketing really result in lower cost of distribution.
3. Lower price to consumer mean a real increase in the national income.
4. Marketing provides new verities of useful and quality goods to consumers.

5. This raises the standard of living of people.
6. Marketing offers wider employment opportunities.
7. Marketing converts yesterday Luxuries into today's necessaries.
8. Marketing is connecting link between the consumer and the producer. Marketing process brings new and new items to retail shops, from where the consumer can have them.
9. Marketing helps in increasing the living standard of people. Because of mass production costs of manufacturing and marketing have come down. This facilitates the fixing of cheaper rates and is a boon to the society. Thus reduction in price will result in a higher standard of living.
10. Marketing removes the imbalances of supply by transferring the surplus to deficit areas, through better transport facilities.

Review Questions

From your knowledge of the material in this chapter, give brief answers to the following questions below.

1. What are the principal differences between marketing domestically and internationally or globally?
2. What factors have led to the growth of "Internationalism" since World War II? Discuss which you think are the most important and why.
3. Which concepts and techniques are available to aid marketers isolate differences and similarities in domestic and international marketing in order for them to plan appropriate marketing strategies?
4. Explain the objectives and importance of global marketing?

2 Functions of Global Marketing

Marketing involves certain activities to make the goods to start Journey from the place of production to the place of consumption.

Pyle has classified the marketing functions into two major groups–concentration and dispersion. The classification is shown below:

The act of operation and services which are concerned with the marketing activities are called marketing functions.

The global marketing function has been evolved from Clark and Clark definition. The global marketing functions under three major functions under three major groups are as follows.

Functions of Exchange

Exchange brings about changes in the ownership of products. It consists three functions.

Buying

It is first step of marketing functions. It is carried out by the manufacturers, wholesalers the retailer and consumers. Buying and selling are inseparable both happen at the same time. Buying implies Business.

Assembling

Assembling is concerned with the collection and concentration of goods of the same type from different sources at a place for further movement. Generally goods are brought from many

Global Marketing Function

Concentration Global Function	*Dispassion of Global Function*
1. Buying or Assembling	1. Selling
2. Transporting	2. Transporting
3. Storing	3. Grading
4. Grading	4. Financing
5. Financing	5. Risk bearing
6. Risk bearing	6. Directing

sellers. When they are purchased from different small producers, Scattered over a wide area, they are to be assembled together at a central place.

Marketing Functions

Function of Exchange	*Function of physical supply*	*Facilitating Functions*
1. Buying	1. Transportation	1. Financing
2. Assembling	2. Storage	2. Risk Bearing
3. Selling		3. Standardisation
		4. Marketing
		5. Promotion

Selling

Selling and buying are complement to each other marketing efforts evolve around the buying and selling functions. In a business, the selling function is many important. The primary objective of marketing is to sell the products at a profit. By selling the ownership is transferred to the buyers.

Functions of Physical Supply

Transportation

As transportation marketing function assumes unique importance because of mass production. Mass distribution and ever widening markets. Markets are geographically separated from production, hence transportation is very essential.

Storage

Storage creates time utility. Products one preserved from the time of consumption. Production may be during particular season, but demand is regular. In the same way, Production may be regular but demand may be only in seasonal time. In both case products have to be stored. Storage function is necessary in concentration as well as in dispersion.

The function is done by the manufacturer wholesalers and professional house keeper. The market can easily adjust supply and demands through the warehousing and transportation. Storage function is performed through warehouse.

Facilitation Functions

Financing

It is very difficult to carry marketing activities smoothly without the availability of adequate and cheap finance, Commercial bonds, Co-operative credit societies and government agencies arranges for short-term finance to facilitate marketing.

Risk Bearing

Marketing of goods involves innumerable risk due to theft, accidents. The most important factor responsible for the risk is fluctuation in price. The other factor may be changes in the habit of consumers, natural calamities etc.

Businessmen have to for see the business risks and take concrete steps to avoid such a risk like insurance. Still there are risks which are to be borne by the businessmen.

Standardization

Standardization is related with the division of commodities into distribute groups standard is used in providing certain basic qualities to the goods for their use. It is "Norm" grade, or category.

Standards are fixed on the physical characteristics of products. The standardized product possess uniform characteristics. For example shape, weight, size etc. Grading applies certain qualitative specification. For example grading of fruits, agricultural produces etc. According to their size colour, juice content, taste etc. Grading starts where standardization ends, that is standardization proceeds grading.

Market Information

The desired success of marketing depends on correct and timely decisions. These decisions are based on market information or market intelligence. The customer's wants, habits, purchasing power etc. are to be considered, the strength or weakers of competitors' trend in market, supply, and demand etc. are to be taken into account. Market, information includes all facts, estimates, opinions and other information used in making decision which affects the marketing of products or services.

Most of the decisions of business firms are based on the interpretation of available data.

Promotion

Promotion is a wide term including advertising, personal selling, sales promotion etc. Marketing communication are essential for both sellers and buyers. Sales promotion are marketing device to stimulate or re-stimulate for products. The behaviour of buyers can favorably be influenced only through promotion. Promotional programmes are needs for both consumers goods and industrial goods.

Persuasive communication or effective promotion will facilitate the marketers to increase and maintain their market shares.

Clasification of Transport

History and Development:

Classification of Transport

(i) Land

(ii) Water

(iii) Air (Aero plane)

Land

1. Road ways
2. Railways
3. Trans Ways
4. Pipelines

Road Ways

(a) Man (Head Load, Hand cart)

(b) Animals (Bullock, Carts, Tonga's)

(c) Automobiles (Motor cars, Buses, Trucks, Lorries)

Railways

(a) Trains (Steam, Diesel, Electricity)

(b) Piggy-Back

Water

1. Inland water ways
2. Ocean Ways

Inland Water Ways

(a) Canals

(b) River

(c) Channels

(d) Lakes

(Canoes, Rafts, Boats small ships)

Ocean Ways

(a) Coastal

(b) Overseas

(Ships liners and passenger tramps, Tankers, industrial carriers containers, Fishy-back, ships,).

Air (Aero plane)

1. Internal
2. International

International

(a) Cargo flight

(b) Passengers

Land Transport

Road Transport

Merits

1. Cheap hers
2. Safety
3. Flexibility
4. Wider Coverage
5. Serves rural areas
6. Less pricing
7. Sources of implement

Demerits

1. Irregular Operation
2. Limited carrying capacity
3. Slow speed
4. Rates

Rail Transport

Merits

1. Most suitable for heavy and bulky commodities
2. Long distance travel
3. Cheap rate
4. High speed
5. Employment opportunity

Demerits

1. Lesser accessibility
2. Inflexibility
3. Not suitable for local transport

4. Huge Maintenance expenditure
5. Inconvenient for rural and all area.

Water Transport

Merits

1. Cheapest means
2. Carrying capacity
3. Creator of international Trade
4. Especially suitable for certain areas

Demerits

1. Low speed
2. Seasonal difficulties
3. Longer Journey required
4. Dependence on climates conditions
5. Limited area operation

Air Transport

Merits

1. Rapid speed
2. No–barriers
3. Boon to perishable commodities
4. Regular and comfortable
5. Suitable for valuable goods
6. Spray of insecticides
7. Emergency remedies
8. Reduce capital investment

Demerits

1. High rate
2. Low carrying capacity

3. Dependence on climate condition
4. High rate of accident.
5. Needs a high Degree of Training.
6. Low and Restrictions.
7. Suitable only to costly goods.
8. Not flexible

Mode of Transport

There are merits and demerits for each mode of transport. The marketer must prefer the transport system which is economical and convenient for him.

The marketing manager must select the appropriate decide by considering the following factors.

1. Usefulness or contribution of modes.
2. Specific carriers.
3. Own or lease transportation.

The management or marketer on must consider the following points.

1. Suitability
2. Cost
3. Safety
4. Flexibility
5. Regularity
6. Availability

Storage

What is Storage?

Storage can be defined as one of the marketing functions involving preservation of goods between the time of products and the time of consumption.

It is a process of holding and preservation of production and demand for it, as long as the production continues.

Storage is essential to protect the goods carried over from determination in order to use them in the period of scarcity and also it adds to the depth of market storing of goods are essential for transportation and transportation follows storing, this is called physical distribution.

Situation Requires Storage

The need of storage arises fundamentally due to lack of adjustment between times of consumption. The storage of products becomes necessary in the following cases.

1. Seasonal production but uniform consumption.
2. Uniform production but seasonal consumption.
3. Protection of goods.
4. To maintain balance between demand and supply.

Warehouses

Meaning

It is a place where the goods are stored is known as warehouse. Warehouse implies a house for wares. A ware means products.

The term ware means articles or merchandise collectively or a go down is a room or a building for the accumulation of goods possessing facilities to person other marketing functions.

Functions

Warehouses perform the following functions which are essential in the process of marketing.

1. Warehouse is a convenient resting place of surplus goods which are produced in seasonal periods and made available to the market when needed.
2. Ware house assumes the responsibility to care for the goods of internet quality free from deterication due to daimatic changes.
3. Ware house keeper accepts the responsibility based on bailment Act. It means warehoused goods are lost or damaged or destroyed the warehouse–keeper–has

to reimburse the less i.e. risk is transferred by the producer.

4. Warehouse receipts help the owners of the goods get finance from the banker by pledging them.
5. Ware house keeper takes the responsibility of mixing, grading and packing at the direction of producer.

Kinds of Warehouse

On the Basis of Place of Necessity

In-plant Warehouse

This kind of warehouse is located within the factory i.e. now-a-days must of the manufactured used to have their owner warehouse within their factory for storing of surplus product until the need will arise. So, by way of maintaining their own warehouse, the cost of production can be minimized as much as possible and it gives ways the producer to earn more profit by way of fulfilling the consumer needs at appropriate time.

Field Warehousing or Custodian Warehousing

These are centrally located warehouses where from distribution is done to wholesaler and retailers. All the manufactured products can not be sent immediately after the production is over. In some special circumstance the producer have to preserve their product under custodian ware house instead of storing in their implant. Warehouse for the purpose of obtaining Bank loans and from where the product will be distributed through wholesaler and retailer to the ultimate consumer for which the public warehouse keeper will be custodian.

On the Basis of Ownership

Private Warehouse

A firm or manufacturer or a trader who operates a warehouse exclusively for their own purpose is called a private ware house.

For Example

(a) Inplant warehouse and

(b) Field warehouse

Public Warehouse

This type of warehouse is operated by Government. It may be owned by central or state Government. The general public can use it. The operation system and rates of rent are regulated by government. For which the users have to pay rental charges calculated on basis of area occupied period used and special nature of commodity.

In India the warehouses are controlled by the ware housing corporation Act 1962 and a Central warehouse corporation was established on March 2, 1957. (To look into the warehousing problems).

Co-operative Warehouse

The ownership these houses are in the hands of primary Co-operative society. So far it has not been popular. But if it is properly organized, it is boon to agriculturists in villages.

Specialty Warehouse

Certain products like explosives, have to be stored under special condition, hence to meet this need specialized warehouse came into operations.

Special Commodity Warehouses

These warehouse are constructed especially to save certain commodities which required special treatment.

For Example

Grains, wool and cotton, explosives etc. require special facilities such as maintenance of fixed temperature and non-exposure to light.

Refrigerated Warehouse or Cold Warehouse

This is the latest contribution of technology which made storing functions really capable of giving time utility to any product.

Perishable products are given second life producers are generally benefited by this.

Advantages of Warehousing

1. Public warehouses are built in modern methods. Which reduce all types of losses and safeguard the goods.
2. It eradicate the imbalances between demand and supply.
3. It increases inherent quality of certain types of goods like rice, tobacco, liquor, wine, honey, gur pickles, and cheese.
4. Cold storage facilitates longer life to perishable items, such as fruits vegetables, fish and dairy products.
5. Products may be stored at seasonal time and in non-seasonal times, the products fetch good prices.
6. It facilitates for continuous sales.
7. It provides employment opportunities to millions of people.
8. Financial aid can be made available against goods stored as a collateral security.
9. Storage is necessary to carry out other marketing function. Such as grading, cleaning, mixing and packing.
10. Almost all the form products produced seasonally are in demand through out the year so, it facilitates producer to preserve their product in it.
11. Some types of goods are demanded seasonally and their production is uniform. These goods must be stored in order to affect timely supply to meet heavy demand.

Standardisation

Meaning

Standardization means the establishment of certain standards on the qualities or the intrinsic physical properties of a commodity. The standard is determined on the basis of size, colour flavour, appearance, strength etc. It involves setting up of standards and maintaining those standards for the products.

The standard product carries the ideas of uniformity. It means and implies that a standardized product brought from different seller is the same.

Definition

Duddy and Razan define "Standardization is the process of determining of classes or grader of a product or service that have fixed limits.

Meaning

Standards are ideal or model products which provide a basis for comparison with identical products. In other words, standards convey the idea of uniformity and identity in respect of quality or quantity or some other matters.

Standardization is the process by which a standard already decided is attained.

Types of Standards

Standards are determined on the basis of certain fundamental characteristics of the product. There are three types of standard. They are as follows.

Quantity Standard

Weights and measures are the standards usually used for the determination of quantity.

Standardization of weights and measures and enforcement of them are under the responsibility of central and state governments and local bodies. The standard weights and measures are kilogram, Meter, Litre.

Standards of Size and Measurement

The standards are determined on the basis of the size of the product.

For Example

Ready made garments, shoes, thread, nut, bolt, pipe. Such products are purchased and sold on the basis of size and measurement.

Quality Standard

This standards depends on the prescription of customers and users however, having product differentiations and positive quality are the basis of standardizing really which is difficulty to be established.

Positive Standard

The standards which express positive the qualities present in the product.

Negative Standard

The standards which express positive the qualities absent in the product.

General Standard

They relate to all similar commodities no matter who produce them.

Private Standards

Standards are private when an individual's manufacturer limits or prescribes certain standards for his products.

For Example

Term for cloths is a general standard and liberty shirts a private standard.

Grading

Meaning

Grading means sorting out the products in homogeneous groups on the basis of their common characteristics such as size, quality, colour, type.

Grading actually starts where standardization ends. Standards determines the quality of products whereas grading divides the product into uniform group according to certain standards of size, colour, shape etc.

Definition

Touky Clark and Clark have defined the term as "To grade is to divide into lots which have approximately the same characteristics as type, size or quality that is to sort products into the standards grades to which they belong".

Advantages of Standardization and Grading

1. It helps to protect products in transit from damage and reduce the cost of marketing by achieving economy in freight and handling.
2. Standardized goods require less storage area. This reduces storage charges.

Review Questions

1. Explain in detail about functions of exchange.
2. Discuss about the functions of physical supply.
3. Explain the functions of facilitating.

3 Promotional Methods of Global Marketting

Meaning

Promotional mix or methods are adopted to increase sales. The activities are done in order to increase the sales of product or services.

Purpose of Promotion

There three specific purposes of promotion.

1. To Communicate
2. To convince and
3. To compete

Need for Communication

When a company develops a new product changes in old one or to increase sales of an existing product. It must be communicated, Therefore promotion involves in communication in the marketing for increasing sales.

For Convincing

The purpose of promotional activities not only the communication of information but also to convince the customers to buy the product. Which means the distribution of information should be capable of producing marketing result.

To Compete

A good product, an efficient channel and appropriate price are not enough to get success in the market but also communication and convincing elements should be supplement to offer to efforts of the competitors, then only they can exist in the market.

Objectives of Promotion

Promotion is the mode of communication adopted by business community for achieving certain specific objectives. Such as to modify consumer behaviour and thoughts or to reinforce existing behaviour of consumer.

Global Advertising

Advertising is the activity by which visual or oral messages are addressed to the general public in order to increase the sales of advertiser, It is done with a view to sell the goods or services offered by the advertiser. (It may also draw the reader's or viewer's attention to act favourably towards the idea or placed in advertisement. The aim is to persuade people to create desire for new product).

Advertising is any paid form of non personal presentation of goods or ideas by an identified sponsor.

Definition

1. Little fields defined it as "Advertising is mass communication of information intended to persuade buyers to maximize profit.
2. Hall defines it as "Selesmenship in writing print or pictures or spreading information by means of the written and printed word and the pictures.

Kinds of Global Advertising

Product Advertising	*Institutional Advertising*
(a) Informative or primary demand or advertising	1. Informative pioneer
(b) Competitive or selective advertising	2. Persuasive
	3. Reminder

(c) Reminder advertising
(d) Shortage advertising
(e) Co-operative advertising
(f) comparative advertising.
(g) Commercial advertising.

Informative and Primary Demand

This kind of advertising is given to inform about the products and services and also o create demand when it is introduced in the market initially.

Selective or Competitive Advertising

When a product enters growth stage of the life cycle where competition begins, to avoid this a company must select a suitable advertising to compete with competitor is called, selective or competitive advertising.

Comparative Advertising

These type of advertising stress on comparative features of two or more, specific brands in the terms of product or services. It is used in the maturity stage when similar products fastly appearing in the market, which brings a stiff competition.

Shortage Advertising

It is adopted when shortage in the supply of products but high demand.

Objectives of this advertising are:

(a) Educating the users of more efficient of utilising the product to reduce demand.
(b) To reduce the customer pressure on sales force.
(c) Making appeal to save resource.

Co-Operative Advertising

Its jointly sponsored by manufacturer, whole saler and retailer and expenditures are also jointly sponsored by them to increase sale is called Co-operative advertising.

Commercial Advertising

It is also termed as business advertising which consist the following types.

Industrial Advertising

It is exclusively used for selling industrial products.

Trade Advertising

Advertising relate to trade.

Professional Advertising

Undertaken by professional people such as doctor, accountants, Lawyers and Engineers.

Farm Advertising

Exclusively used for selling farm products such as fertilizers, and insecticides. some kind of specialization is found in all the above form of advertising. Hence all these forms could be commonly called as selective advertising. Selective advertising sometime used to denote such advertisements that stress a particular products. e.g. Fiat Car.

Institutional Advertising

It is not only used to direct consumer alone but also it is aimed at many of the various sets of public like shareholders and creditors. It is not at all product oriented, but also designed to change the image of the company which consist three types, they are as follows.

1. Informative advertising
2. Persuasive advertising
3. Reminder advertising

Advantages of Global Advertising

Advantages to Manufacture

(a) It increases the sales value by creating attraction towards product.

(b) It helps easy introduction of new products into the markets by same manufacturer.

(c) It helps to create image and reputation.

Not only the products but also of the advertiser. In this way it creates good will for the manufacturers product.

(d) It helps to controls product price:

By the advertisement the wholesaler and retailer prices can be controlled by conveying price to consumers.

(e) It maintain the existing market shares:

The advertisement can help the advertiser to retain old customer consequently the old existing market share can be maintained.

Advantages to Wholesalers and Retailers

1. Easy sale of the products is possible since consumers are aware of product and its quality.
2. *Increases the turnover:* Advertising helps quick sales product which is in turn increases the rate of return of product.
3. *It attracts more customer:* It attracts more customers in the particular shop by way of giving detailed information about the product and the availability of the product at particular shop.
4. *Economic selling:* Advertising ensures more economic selling.

Advantages to Consumers

Easy Purchasing

Advertising helps customers in easy purchasing of the products by way of giving usual information about the price and quality of products.

There are many tablets for headache like anacin, aspro, coldreine, at a good advertising can help in buying the best one.

Connecting Link

It connects the link between consumer and manufacturer and also in eliminate middlemen. There is no profit for the middlemen. Hence the price is low.

Fair Price

It helps the customers to get the product at fair price.

Save Time

It helps customers by giving information about the availability of product i.e. where and when, hence the consumer can select best product in a particular shop, thus reduce their shopping time.

Educates the Customer

The aim of advertising is to educate the customers about the introduction of new products.

Advantages to Community

Increase Employment Opportunities

Advertising generate employment opportunity directly and indirectly direct employment opportunities advertising on artists, painters, singers, musicians, writers, photographers, pressmen, and managing agencies.

It creates mass sales followed by mass production which in turn opens the door for more employment indirectly.

Uplifts Standard of Living

Advertising is an effecting tool which raises the standard of living of people of advanced countries. The standard of living is measured by the amount of national income and its distribution and consumption pattern. Advertising gives stimulus to the consumers to buy new variety of products. It leads to large-scale production of more varieties of products followed by mass consumption. Thus advertising creates a demand for standardised product.

Advertisement Copy

Meaning

The basic functions of advertising i.e. influencing and motivating people is done through the advertising copy.

The words used to convey the advertising ideas are called the copy. An analysis of advertisement reveals that most of the fails for want of a good copy of advertisement. It is observed that the aim of advertising copy is that it shall be seen and read the messages conveyed and then acted upon.

Functions of a Good Advertisement Copy

1. It must make people to see it.
2. It must make people to read it.
3. It must make people to understand it.
4. It must make people to believe it.
5. It must make people to buy the product.

Elements of an Advertisement Copy

The advertisement must have the following values acceptable to the consumers and capable of attracting them.

1. Attention value.
2. Suggestive value.
3. Conviction value.
4. Sentimental value
5. Educational value
6. Memorizing value
7. Instinct value.
8. Action value.

Attention value

People are very busy, they find time very rarely almost all the people, who are able to make a purchase but they do not have enough time, under this situation the advertisement must be able to attract the attention of readers, at a glance. There must be some specialty in the advertisement to make it more attractive. The attraction can be created through following device.

(a) Pictures and drawings should have direct effects on products.

(b) The head line must be good with proper border.

(c) It must have a pleasing colorful presentation.

(d) It should not be congested i.e. these must have enough inter-space.

(e) Slogans must be lively.

Suggestive Value

The advertising copy should give useful information to those who go through the advertisement.

Conviction Value

The advertisement should never be misleading it means, the statement in the advertisement must be genuine and accurate. Misrepresentation and exaggerative words mostly be avoided Simple and plain words can have effect on readers to convince them to buy the product then colorful and flattering words.

The pictures, drawings or the painting should corroborate the facts.

For Example

1. To get Relax–Smoke a charminar.
2. To get excitement drink, Bru coffee.

Suggestive Value

The advertisement should suggest the advantage of buying a particular product.

For Example

1. ONIDA TV–Owners pride neighbours envy.
2. BPL–Believe in Best.

3. Don't talk about the weather even in the hottest summer– Just install a Blue star air conditioner.
4. Intel Pentium Processor based PC. can make your business more really fast. Now if you too more really fast you can get them at new low price with great offers.
5. Memorizing value.

The advertisement should leave a strong feelings and lasting impressions on the reader's mind. For this purpose the advertisement have to be repeated frequently and even the first advertisement should be capable of making the reader remember the product image.

For Example

1. Horlicks gives extra energy.
2. Glaxo, build bonnic babies.

Memerising value can be created by using symbols and brand names.

Sentimental Value

While preparing advertising copy the advertiser should consider the likes dislikes and wishes of readers it means, the advertiser should respect the sentiments and feelings of people for whom it is given instead of insulting them.

Educational Value

When products are manufactured for the first time, it is the duty of the producer through advertisements to draw the attention of the people and to tell them usage, merits, ingredient and special features of product. These can be achieved through the educational value, hence while preparing advertisement copy the advertiser should consider educational value.

Instinct Value

It is a psychological problem. The human behavior is fundamentally related to instinct. This instinct makes the people behave differently at different times. So according to their behavior the people will buy different product at different times.

Action Value

If the advertising copy has action value it can make people act to buy product.

Selection of Suitable Advertising Media

Selection of advertising media is most fundamental duty of manufacturer or advertiser. Because the success of manufacturer completely depends on advertisement. If he fail to select right media those can satisfy the following objectives, (1) It has to reach maximum prospects, (2) It must gain the affection of readers and (3) It must have wide coverage at less cost.

The Selection of Media Must Be Based on the Following Factors

Objective of Advertisement

The manufacturer should consider, the objective of advertising for media selection. It influenced both by the purpose of a specific advertisement and goals of entire campaign.

For the goal of campaign is to generate appointment for salesmen, direct mail is suitable, If it is to include to public with in a day or two, newspaper, Radio, TV may be used.

Media Circulation

Every medium has general circulation. The medium is to be selected which will reach the market with minimum waste circulation.

The Cares of People

The manufacturer should find out the people, to whom, he will give advertisement, than he can select media according to them. The medium is to be selected by the kind of customers sex, age, cultural, social, educational standard etc. again urban groups or rich and poor, hence the media mist be according to them.

For Example

If the products are for young people better select radio or newspaper. If the product are for grown ups then sales letters will be followed.

Business Unit

Selection of media is affected by the size and the nature of the business unit. It may be a departmental store or large firms makes use of radio. TV or Newspaper. Whereas small firms makes use of cinema slides and posters.

Message to be sent

The medium should fit the message.

Cost of Space

Cost of the advertising media should be considered in relation to funds available for circulation of media. The larger circulation the higher rates charged. Preferred positions are charged at higher rates and so is the case with advertisements in colour.

The advertiser should try to develop some relationship between the cost of the medium and the size of audience.

Review Questions

1. Discuss the process of promotions.
2. Discuss the meaning and different types of advertising.
3. Explain the advantages and disadvantages of advertising.
4. Write meaning and different values of advertisement copy.
5. Explain different factors for selecting suitable advertising medias.

4 Personal Selling of Global Marketting

Meaning

Personal selling is the method of communication. It involves individual and social behavior. Each person is contacted by face to face conversation. Personal selling influences the buyers to buy a product. Personal selling reaches the goal of marketing offer i.e. to increase profitable sales.

Definition

Rover Louis Stevenson stated "Everyone living by selling something". The people who do selling are called salesmen, sales representatives, sales person's account executives, sales consultants, sales engineers, field representatives, agents, service representative, marketing representative etc.

Personal selling and salesmanship used without distinction. But there are some difference between the two.

According to Philip Kotler "The personal selling involves oral presentation in a conversation with one or more prospective purchaser for the purpose of making sales".

Objectives of Personal Selling

There are two objectives.

1. Long term and
2. Short term

Long Term

1. To do the entire job.
2. To save the existing customer.
3. To search out and obtain new customer.
4. To secure and obtain customer's Co-operation in stock and promoting the product line.
5. To keep customers informed of changes in the product line.
6. To assit the customer in selling the product line.
7. To provide technical advice and assistance to customers.
8. To handle the sales personnel of middlemen.
9. To provide advice and assistance to middlemen whenever needed.
10. To collect and report market information to company management.

Short Term

1. To obtain specified sales volume.
2. To obtain sales volume in ways that contributes profit objectives, by selling proper price of products.
3. To keep personal selling expenses with in specified limit.
4. To secure and retain specified share of market.

Sales promotion techniques are indirect and non-personal while personal selling are quiet direct and personal.

The main purpose of the sales promotion activities is to stimulate consumers and dealers.

Sales promotion directed at consumers may be done with a view to increase the usage rate of products among existing consumers or to attract new consumers.

Promotional activities may be in some promotional scheme such as samples demonstration, coupons, contest etc. or in store promotional scheme such as temporary price reduction, premium offers, demonstration etc. Dealers promotional activities include cash discount on purchase display and advertisement allowances, prices and gifts fee products. etc.

The Nature of Personal Selling

1. Personal selling is a process of informing customers and persuading them to purchase products through personal communication in an exchange situation.
2. Personal selling is a component element in the communication mix.
3. It is a two way form of communication that has number of advantages from the view point of marketing organisation. They are as follows.
   (a) Personal selling gives marketers the greatest freedom to adjust a message to satisfy customers' information need.
   (b) In comparison with other promotion methods, personal selling is the most precise, enabling marketers to focus on the most promising sales prospectus.
4. It is also vital not to concentrate solely on today's products, customers and problems but to think in terms of where future sales will be coming from.

Qualities of Salesman

Physical Qualities

Good Appearance

The outward appearance of salesman makes some impression on the customers. The salesman can make him good appearance by neat dress with pleasing appearance and finally it make him get success.

Sound Health

Sound health and good physique are very essential for salesman. The salesmen should maintain sound health because they have to travel to many place, for eating different varieties of food, to face different kinds of weather conditions. Health is wealth. A salesman who lacks a healthy body, is unable to give a good appearance and fails to carryout his duties.

Pleasing Voice

The voice is very important for a salesmen. It must be attractive. It should not irritate the customers. The voice should not be like that of a horse or donkey.

Mental Qualities or Psychological Qualities

Quick Action

A salesman must be alert and quick in action. He must have the mentality to face any situation and be ready to answer any questions. He must have quick thought of answering what to say, how to tell, and how to tackle the situation.

Self Confidence

Confident man never fails. As salesman, they should have confidence on their ability and skill. Confidence makes them optimistic and enthusiastic and it can make them to meet any situation.

Enthusiasm

It makes salesman more pleasant and also it gains interest and confidence of buyers and increase more sales.

Creative Talks

The salesman talk should be creative one.

Observation

A Salesman should have a keen observation. He must have up-to-date knowledge of his products and changes in style and fashions, and attitudes of customers and competitors and government, to make his clever salesman.

Social Qualities

Good manners

As a salesman they should cultivate good manners. Good manners are charming while bad manners are irrigative.

Annoyed replies and irritated actions will sweep away them from their duty persons having good manners can do their duty very easily.

Courtesy

Using polite and courteous words a sales-man can walk away very easily to achieve his duty. By using pleasing words like thank you please excuese me will make him win heart of the customers.

Tactfulness

When a delicate situation is faced a tactful salesman can deal with it in proper way. Through tactfulness, one can avoid obstacles and troubles.

Helpfulness

A Salesmen's decent behavior, courtesy, attentive attitude are the base for politeness, customers feel satisfaction through the polite dealings of salesmen.

Friendliness

A salesman must be able to give grand welcome to all those who have come to the shop with friendly.

Moral Qualities

Determination

A salesman must have constant effort and patience in his profession to improve further.

Sincerity

He must be sincere towards his assigned duties by being sincere one can win friends, enroll new customers retain old customer and win similar other favours.

Integrity

It denotes honesty trust and purity. The talks and behavior of a salesman must be believed, trusted, honored and agreed by others.

Loyalty

A salesman must have a full desire to work in co-operation with the firm by adopting the policies laid down by the firm.

Courage

This is quality that enables one to meet danger without giving way to fear, as a salesman they should have bravery and boldness to face any situation.

Self Management

A self governed salesman can meet any number of customers. Therefore, he must plan work in advance and he work according to plan. Such a salesman find enough time and has a feeling of self assurance.

In addition to the above qualities he should have the following qualities also.

1. Knowledge of self.
2. Knowledge of product.
3. Knowledge of firm.
4. Knowledge of customers.
5. Knowledge of competition.
6. Knowledge about market.
7. Knowledge of selling techniques.
8. Personal attributes.

Types of Salesman

Creative Salesman

As the name suggest, the job of such a salesman emphasises the creation of demand for the product. They are otherwise called missionary salesman on account of missionary nature of work. He is also called a pioneer salesman since it is he who pioneers the market for product. Generally they are engaged in developing customers and sales territories.

Service Salesman

Such kind of salesman specialises in selling intangible products like insurance, shares, advertising space or travelling arrangements.

Detail Salesman

The names detail selling and detail salesman are the contribution of drug industry. Drug industry produces the products first and then create a demand. The job of detail salesman is not to contact the consumers directly but they call on physician who is the agency instrumental in selling the product because the customer does not purchase the product at his own but purchase only on the prescription of the physician.

Manufacturer's Salesman

The salesman directly appointed, controlled and paid by manufacturer is known as Manufacturer's salesman.

The main job of such kind of salesmen is to see that the dealers are well satisfied with regard to the regular flow of goods.

Wholesalers Salesman

A wholesaler is an intermediary and occupies a vital position in the channel of distribution. He is the nerve centre of distribution he has to push the goods to retailers. The retailers are geographically scattered hence he might require the services of a salesman to have contact with them the person those who involved between wholesaler and retailer is called wholesaler's salesman.

Generally the following services are rendered by wholesaler's salesman.

(a) Regularly meeting retailers for the distribution of goods receiving complaints and collection of bills.
(b) Guiding the wholesaler in extending credit to retailers.
(c) Colleting the information about markets competition.
(d) Establishing liaison between retailers and customers.
(e) Helping retailer to arrange display and demonstration.

Retailer's Salesman

Salesmen employed by retailers is called retailer salesman. They are two types.

Indoor Salesman

The salesman whose area operation is limited within four walls of the shop, i.e. at the shop of retailers. He is also termed as a counter salesman. His job is to sell the articles to the customers over the counter.

Outdoor Salesman

It is opposite to indoor salesman. The nature of work of such kind of salesman is to move from place to place. He is also called traveling salesman.

Specialty Salesman

Specialty articles are generally high priced and purchases are made only after personal selection by the buyers and they are not bought regularly and are durable goods.

Eg.: Car, Refrigerator.

This requires the specialty salesman to have a considerable amount of initiative drive and product knowledge to sell them.

Staple Salesman

Staple articles are those articles which are common in use such as food items, stationary and clothes. Therefore, staple salesman are those who are busy in selling staple goods.

Exporter's Salesman

The foreign trade involves a large number of problems on account of different nationalities different currency etc. The greatest among the problem is to find market for the product where the manufacturer has no way. From early times special agencies known as "indent house" have been working in this field. They act as an agent as well as middlemen for a manufacturer. The import of goods also such indent house render valuable service.

Is Salesmanship an Art or Science

The suffix ship generally mean skill or art. In addition selling is often described as a creative art. Some kinds of salesman are even referred to as creative salesman.

All the above give way for a strong belief that salesmanship is an art. This belief was supported by the idea that a salesman will have to meet people with different mentalities, moods and temperaments and he can not apply to everyone standardised set of rules based on systematise knowledge would simply fail in such circumstances. Moreover an art is described as a process of producing result by the exercise of skill.

Today salesmanship could be conducted not merely by possessing certain skills but such skills should be polished with proper amount of training. The training of course is scientifically based. This is more evident in the following word salesmen are neither born nor made.

There should be latent quality in a salesman but this alone is not enough such qualities must be given shape with the application of scientific rules.

The knowledge is to be acquired by a salesman in order to prove himself fit and successful in the field. It is often remarked that experience is a great assets for salesmanship. But acquisition of experience is time consuming process, some time requiring a whole life period. Hence training is more essential for salesmanship for giving more knowledge within short period and to achieve result within right time and stipulated time.

Therefore salesmanship is neither a form of art nor is completely based on scientific knowledge it is combination of both. A salesman should have inborn talents and must have real interest in the profession.

Selling as an art requires patient practice and use of correct methods. As a science it requires mastery over certain fundamentals that are prerequisites for success in selling.

Advertising and Publicity

Advertising is defined as any paid form of non-personal presentation and promotion of ideas, goods or services by an identified sponsor.

Publicity has been defined by AMA as "non-personal" stimulation of demand for product, service or business unit by planting commercially significant news about it in published medium or obtaining a favourable presentation of it on radio, television or stage that is not paid by the sponsor "The advertiser has to pay for advertisement. In case of publicity, it is not necessary.

For Example: In election, the expenses of popularising a candidate may or may not be paid by the candidate.

Advertising is a purposeful attempt sponsored by party whereas publicity may or may not be sponsored by the party. It means the person passing massage may not come to the stage.

Advertising is a method of publicity. In other words publicity involves a number of methods including advertising.

Review Questions

1. Define personal selling and its objectives.
2. Explain qualities of salesman.
3. Discuss the different types of salesman.

5 Global Sales Promotion

Origin

The word promotion originate from the Latin word 'Promovere' The meaning is to move forward to push forward or to advance an idea. The aim of production is sales, sales and promotion are two different words and sales promotion is the combination of these two words. Sales promotion increase the sales.

Definition

According to AMA, "Sales promotion is those marketing activities other than personal selling, advertising and publicity, that stimulate consumer purchasing and dealer effectiveness such as display showrooms, exhibition, demonstration and other non-recurrent selling efforts not in ordinary routine".

Advantages of Global Sales Promotion

Low Unit Cost

Sales promotion is always the outcome of Large-scale production. Large scale production reduce the cost per unit of product but this could be achieved only with appropriate method of large scale selling.

Effective Sales Support

Basically sales promotion policies support and supplement the effort of personal selling and advertising. It means it makes salesman effort more productive.

Increased Speed of Product Acceptance

Most of the sales promotion devices like contest premia and coupon are used faster than the other promotion methods such as advertisement.

Better Control

The management has effective control over the various methods used. The financial aspects also could be brought under perfect control of the management.

For Example: Cost of sales promotion can be compared with the profit per unit of the product sold.

Limitations of Global Sales Promotion

1. There is a feeling that such seasonal sales promotion activities are mainly intended to sell on inadequate product.
2. That such discount is not real since the price of product already inflated. i.e. discount has been already included in price of product
3. These activities are short lived.
4. It is short run tool used to stimulate immediate increase in demand.

Tools or Devices of Sales Promotion

I Consumer Promotion	*II Middlemen Promotion*	*III Sales Force Promotion*
1. Free samples	1. Buying allowance discount	1. Bonus to sales firm
2. Coupons	2. Buy back allowances	2. Contests.
3. Premium or bonus offer	3. Display and advertising allowances	3. Sales meetings conferences
4. Money refund offer	4. Dealer listed promotion	
5. Price off offer	5. Push money	
6. Contest	6. Sales contest	
7. Demonstration	7. Free Gifts	
8. After sales service	8. Credit facility	

Consumer Promotion

Consumer Promotions are used to encourage the customer directly by manufacturer to purchase more company's product then the competitor's product. They are mentioned below.

Free Samples

Free samples are given to customer to increase their interest to buy more products. They are also given to introduce new product and expand market. It is an effective devices when the product is purchased often.

Example: Soap, Detergent, Tea and coffee.

Coupons

Coupon is certificate that entitles the customer to specified saving on the purchase of a specified product. The purpose is to attract the customers and bring them to a particular shop to increase the sales of a particular brand.

Premium or Bonus Offer

It is a temporary price reduction which increases the interest of buyers. Products are offered free or at a reduced cost as an inducement for purchasing.

It is offered to consumers for consumer goods like soap, brush, paste washing powder etc.

For Example: When the customer buys two soaps. a soaps box is given free along with the soaps.

Money Refund Offer

This offer is generally stated in media advertising that the manufacturer will return the price if the product is not to the satisfaction of the customer within a stated period.

Price off Offer

Or Temporary Price Reduction or Bargain offer. This involves an offer to customers of a certain amount of money off the regular price of a product. This is done to attract consumers of other brands to his product.

Contest or Consumer Sweepstakes

The contests are arranged with view to attract new uses to the company's product. An opportunity under this devices is given to customer to contest with a chance to win cash prizes.

Finally consumers submit their names those who are having interest for inclusion in a list of price winning contest. A ticket like a lottery ticket is given to the customer of a specified brand. At the specified time, lots will be drawn. The prize winner get the prize. This system is followed by retail businessmen to promotes sales.

Demonstration

It is the instructions given the customers in the manner of using product.

It is used to attract the attention of the customers. When products are complex and of a technical nature, demonstration is necessary.

Example: Computers and electrical pumping.

After Sales Service

Under this method the producer gives a guarantee to the customers to maintain the product for a certain specified period.

Middlemen Sales Promotion

Buying Allowance Discount

Buying allowance discount is given to the dealers to induce them to buy the manufacturer's product. Such discount may be either deducted on invoice price or cash price.

Buy Back Allowance

This kind of allowances are given to middlemen by manufacturer's to buy manufacturer product regularly and continuously from particular shop or from manufacturer directly.

Display and Advertising Allowances

This allowance is offered to the dealer to display the manufacture's product. The allowance is given on the basis of space provided to display manufacturer's product in the shop.

Dealer-listed Promotion

Under this method dealer name and address is given on the advertisement and other publicity material as calendars, diaries etc., and also it gives a list of dealers or retailers who stock the product or who are engaged in its promotion.

For Example: The advertisement of Bombay dyeing in newspapers carries the name of stockiest of their products.

Push Money (PM)

This is incentive payment in cash or in kinds to the retailer or salesman to push the sale at a fixed rate for each article sold.

Sales Contest

It is device used to stimulate and motivate distributors, dealers and their sales staff. They are offered cash prizes for those who will win the sales contest i.e. who will make the highest sales of the company's Product. In view of the winning chance, in the contest.

Free Gifts

Under this method, producer gives free gifts to the dealer on the basis of quantity of product purchased by him.

Credit Facility

The producers allow credit to their dealers based on quantity purchased by him. This enable them to purchase bulk quantity.

Sales Force Promotion

Bonus to Sales Force

The Manufacturer sets a target of sales for a year for selling shop. If the selling shops sell the product above the targeted sales, the bonus is offered to them.

Sales Force Contests

To increase the interest and efforts of selling shop by sales force over a specified time, these contests are announced. The prizes are given to the salesman who secures the maximum sales in sales contests.

Salesman Meetings and Conferences

These are conducted by manufacturers for the purpose of educating, in spiring and rewarding the salesman. New products and new selling techniques are described and discussed in such meetings.

Review Questions

1. Explain different types of consumer sales promotions.
2. Explain different types of middleman sales promotions.
3. Explain different types of sales force sales promotions.

6 Segmentation of Global Marketing

Meaning

The market segmentation may be defined as the division of market into groups of segments having similar wants.

Definition

According to Philip Kotler:

"Whenever a market for product or service consist of two or more buyers. The Market is capable of being segment" that is divided into meaningful buyer groups. The purpose of segmentation is to determine differences among buyers which may be consequential in choosing among them or marketing them".

Benefits of Market Segmentation:

1. A more pricly definition of market.
2. A more effective marketing programmed.
3. Better assessment of the competition.
4. Better allocation of resources.

The cost of market segmentation:

Certain cost are to be incurred to arrive at the above benefits. These cost are:

1. Product cost
2. Production cost
3. Promotion cost
4. Inventory cost
5. Management cost.

Bases for Global Market Segmentation

Consumer Personal Characterstics Approach (Product Oriented Approach)	*Consumer Response Behaviour (People Oriented Approach)*
1. Geographic characteristics	Usage pattern
2. Demographic characteristics	Benefit pattern
3. Socio-economic characteristic	Brand Loyalty pattern
4. Psychographic characteristics	Storage pattern
	Use of buyers attitudes motives

Consumer Characteristics Approach

Geographic Characteristics

(a) Place of Residence
(b) Region
(c) Urban, sub-urban, Rural
(d) Size of town, city.

Demographic Characteristics

(a) Sex
(b) Age
(c) Marital status
(d) Family size

Socio-economic Characteristics

Income, Occupation, Religion, Culture, Social class.

Psychographic Characteristics

(a) Personality
(b) Life style
(c) Buying motive

Requirement for Effective Segmentation

There are three methods of making effective segmentation.

Measurability

(a) Demographic
(b) Personality
(c) Life style
(d) Motivation.
(e) Perception.
(f) Attitude.

Accessibility

1. Place
2. Time
3. Area

Substitutability

1. Place
2. Characteristics of consumer.

Review Questions

1. Define segmentation of global marketing.
2. Explain the bases of segmentation of global marketing.
3. Discuss the requirement of segmentation of global marketing.

7 Marketing of Services at International Market

Definition

The American marketing Association define services as "activities, benefits or satisfactions which are offered for sale or are provided in connection with the sale of goods.

The definition points out three kinds of services.

1. The activities that are intangible in nature e.g. Transportation.
2. Benefits purely derived from services. e.g. medical service, insurance services etc.
3. The services obtained along with the buying of a product, e.g. after sales-services or the services rendered by a retailer.

Characteristics of Services

Services have several unique characteristics which often present certain special marketing problems. Hence the decision to be taken for marketing services are entirely different from those made for marketing of products. They are as follows.

Intangibility

Most of the problems faced in the marketing of services are due to the intangible nature of services. That mean it can not be touched, seen but it can be felt and measured.

The service firm selling an idea and not a product, hence it must tell the buyers what the service will do. It is usually unable to illustrate, demonstrate or display the service in use. Finally intangibility makes the promotion of service difficult and it is practically impossible to give sample. Consequently, buyers are unable to judge quality and value prior to purchase. Thus the services are bought purely relying on the manufacturer's reputation and the reputation of their salesmen.

Intangibility has certain advantages also. Firstly, there is no problem about its physical distribution.

Secondly there is no warehousing problem it means that there is nothing to store practically. The loses that may arise on account of decline in inventory values also do not affect the service.

Inseparability

In many cases or service can not be separated from the person who sells it. Therefore services are often created and marketed simultaneously.

Example: Electricity is generated and distributed simultaneously.

Perish Ability and Fluctuation in Demand

The utility of most services is short lived. Services can't be produced largely and stored for periods of peak demand. The perishable nature of services is a challenging features for the marketing men unused electrical power, ideal seats in buses or train which is lost for ever to the firm.

Fluctuation in demand pose another problem. The markets for services are often fluctuate usually by seasons and often by day or weak. There is peak period followed by a slack period.

For Example: Telephone department offers connection for using their services during off peak periods. For this special advertising and separate channels of distribution are to utilise.

Absences of Certain Marketing Functions

Services are intangibility and perish ability in nature. Therefore the company those are marketing the services need not depend upon, transportation, storage and warehousing department that means most of the marketing functions are eliminated or reduced here.

Heterogeneity

Services are numerous and it is impossible to standardise the output. The services of even same seller are sometime remarkably dissimilar.

For Example: A Musician has to compose different music for different song according to situation even in the same film.

Customer Relationship

While marketing the services the seller can have direct link with consumer or buyer.

For Example: The doctor–patient relationship.

Lake of Standardisation

Another notable feature of services is that they can not be perfectly standardised like products.

Example: Music can not be standardised for all songs.

Kinds of Services

Personal Services

Many services are personal e.g. house painting and various domestic services.

Facility Services

When products are offered to the customers to provide same facilities, the services may be described as facility services.

For Example: Car, Theatre etc.

Business Services

When Services are rendered to business house they are called business services. These services includes activities such as marketing services, management consultancy services etc.

Customer Services

The services that are offered to ultimate consumers are known as customer services. Such services include laundries, hotels etc.

Difference between Services and Goods

Services	*Goods*
1. Services are often intangible. They may involve acts, deeds, performance efforts. Many services can not be physically possessed. The value of services based on experience.	1. Goods are tangible. They are objects, things materials, value is based on ownership.
2. Services are usually perishable unused capacity can't be stored or shifted from one time to another.	2. Goods can be stored. Surpluses in one period can be applied against shortages in another period.
3. Services are frequently . inseparable One can't separate the quality of many services from the services provided.	3. Goods can be manufactured by one firm and marketed by another. The quality of goods can be differentiated.
4. Services may very in quality overtime it is difficult to standardise.	4. Goods can be standardised. Mass production and quality control can be used

Marketing of Consumer Goods at International Market

Meaning

Goods are known as commodities or products. Goods have been classified into three categories on the basis of consumer needs. They are as follows.

1. Manufactured goods
2. Agricultural goods and
3. Natural raw-materials.

Manufactured Goods

Manufactured goods are these goods that are semi-finished or finished goods used by producers or consumers. Manufactures goods are two types. i.e. (a) Consumer goods and (b) Industrial goods.

Consumer Goods

Consumer goods are those goods which are meant for direct consumption by ultimate consumers and households.

For Example: Car, Television, radio, cycle, shoe, and furniture toys etc.

Industrial Goods

Industrial goods are those goods which are used in the process of manufacturing other goods and services.

For Example: Raw materials, machines, Computers, maintenance supplier etc. and semi-finished goods.

Agricultural Goods

It refers to the produces out of cultivation.

For Example: Vegetables, grain, Fruit, dairy farming, poultry, farming, egg, meat. Of these agricultural goods wheat, rice, pulses etc are food products for human consumption.

Whereas oilseeds, tobacco, cotton etc. are raw-materials for industry. That is these agricultural goods are also classified into industrial goods and consumer goods.

Natural Raw-materials

It is the gift of nature. for Example. Mines, and forest and these are raw-materials which need further operation before use.

Deference between Consumer Goods and Industrial Goods

	Consumer Goods	*Industrial Goods*
1.	Goods bought are meant for consumption	Goods bought are meant for further processing
2.	There is direct demand.	There is derived demand.
3.	Demand is elastic	The demand inelastic
4.	Purchase is made in small lots.	Purchase is made in bulk.
5.	To make purchase ordinary knowledge is enough.	To make purchase, expert knowledge is needed.

Common Goods

Goods which are used for manufacturing other products and services are called industrial goods and goods sold to consumers for direct consumption are consumer goods. But it is important to note certain goods are fall under both categories in industrial and consumer goods. For Example, Papers, type writer, kerosene and computers. etc.

Features of Consumer Goods

Large Scale Production

Consumer goods are manufactured on mass scale because demand for consumer products are quantitatively very high.

The large scale production is also required due to the fact that majority of consumer products are non-durables. All the above factors finally make producer to produce the product continuously and supply the product continuously to the market.

Demand is Primary in Nature

Generally the producers have to go by the demand of consumer because now-a-days marketing is consumer oriented.

Elasticity in Demand

There is no elasticity in essential products such as rice, cloth etc. But there is elasticity in consumer durable goods.

Horizontal Market

It means the product is used many consumers.

For Example: Watches and time-clocks are used by factories, institution and individual etc.

Small Purchase

The unit of purchase is low but frequency of purchase is greater and therefore the total sales are quite high.

Competition

One of the most dusting wishing features of consumer goods is that they are subject to severe competition. This competition may be in price and quality from substitute products to avoid this competition the producer should carry out research on the above area. They should also carryout the research on product life cycle and product mix. In addition to the above, they should maintain brand loyalty to over come competition.

Shifts in Buying Powers

Shifts in population have had tremendous effect upon marketing. There are two shifts that are recognised.

1. The first one is the change of population from village to industrial towns. This migration happens by an attraction for high wages and the city life, consequently this has necessitated some changes in marketing methods. Gradually these markets become saturated.
2. Increase in the income percentage of literacy, the development in transport and communication system power and buying habits have changed the buying power.

Constant Threat from Changes in Fashion

Another peculiar feature of the consumer products is that they are under constant threat from the fashion changes.

People always would like to change their life style according to their educational status, employment status, earning capacity and environments; consequently it will change marketing style repeatedly.

Buying Motive is Emotional

Consumer products are bought purely by emotional impulse status and prestige are more dominant factors than a comparative evaluation of the merits and demerits of the product.

A Housewife buys a refrigerator not purely convinced of its long-term use but for social status gained by owning such a product.

New Classification of Consumer Goods in International Market

Convenience Goods

These goods are bought by consumers frequently, as soon as needed and with minimum shopping effort. They are also made available to the buyers most conveniently at their own places or very near to them and also the consumer has complete knowledge of the particular product and its substitute before he decides to buy most of these goods are non-durable that is they are consumed rapidly. This necessitates frequent purchases and the consumer can neither postpone their purchases nor make them much in advance of the time of consumption.

Example: Cigarettes and petrol.

Shopping Goods

The products that the consumer selects and buys only after making comparison on such bases as suitability, quality, price and style are called shopping goods.

For Example: Furniture and Jewelry.

Specialty Goods

All the luxuries goods which are high priced are called specialty goods.

Example: Television and car.

Insistence Goods

These are goods which may or may not be generally available but for which the consumer refuses to accept any substitute.

For Example: If the consumer wants to buy "Ford Ikon" car and insists on buying only, Ford ikon car. If it is not available they do not like to buy any substitute car, so the ford ikon becomes an insistence goods. This type of goods sometimes included under specialty goods.

Unsought Goods

Products that the consumer does not know about or knows about but does not actively out are referred to as unsought goods.

New products fall under this category until advertising and distribution increase consumer awareness of them.

The goods that need high pressure selling and persuasive advertising are also some times referred to as unsought goods.

Marketing of Industrial Product in Nternational Market

Meaning

Industrial marketing is a set for activities directed toward facilitating and expediting exchanges involving industrial products and customers in industrial market.

Industrial markets consist of commercial manufacturers, government and institutions. They generally buy these products to be used in the production of further products and services for sale or rental to others. These industrial goods may be component parts of other goods.

Classification of Industrial Products

Industrial goods may be classified into seven categories:

1. Raw materials become a part of the final product and are basic materials derived from mines, forms, forests etc.
2. Major equipment includes large machines and tools to undertake production.
3. Accessory equipment consists of standard items used in production and office activities, It does not become a part of the final products like typewriters and computers.
4. Component parts become part of the physical product and either finished items ready for assembly or products that need little processing before assembly like tire, battery for car and lorry.

5. Process materials are used directly production. They are not easily identifiable like component parts in final product like ball bearing, electrical fittings etc.
6. Consumable supplies facilitate a firm's production and operation but do not become actual part of the finished product.

   Example: Paint, Lubricating oil.
7. Industrial services intangible products including consultancy services needs for organisational support.

Marketing of Agricultural Goods in International Market

Meaning

Agricultural marketing is a set of activities directed toward facilitating and expediting exchanges involving agricultural products and consumers in agriculture market.

Classification of Agricultural Goods

We can classify the Agricultural goods into three. They are,

1. Consumer goods.
2. Raw material or Industrial goods.
3. Consumer and industrial goods.

Consumer Goods

Consumer goods are those which can be used by consumers in their natural form without any change by manufacturing process. They are fruits vegetables, egg, milk etc.

Industrial Goods

Raw material for industries. For Example cotton, Jute, Tobacco are used for producing other products are called industrial product or Raw-materials.

Consumer and Industrial Goods

Consumer and industrial goods are those used by both consumers and industries.

When vegetables and fruits are sold to the consumers for consumption purpose then they are called consumer goods.

When they are sold to a canning factor for processing then they are called Industrial goods.

For Example.

Characteristics of Agricultural Goods

Characteristics of agricultural goods can be studied under three heads. They are,

1. Production Characteristics
2. Product characteristics.
3. Consumption Characteristics.

Production Characteristic

Small-Scale Production

Farmers have small holdings of Land. The produce in those Lands is very small which is sufficient for their family needs. If there is any surplus they have to market that more than 75% of the farm products, arriving at the markets are cultivated or produced by small land holders, who cultivate individually.

Catered and Specialised Production

Farmers are scattered over wide area. Some Land is suitable for a particular crop. Different crop need different fertility of the soil different climatic conditions hence some of products can be produced in particular fertility of soil and climatic conditions.

Seasonal Production

Agricultural production is seasonal in character. But there is demand for agricultural goods throughout the year whereas the harvest is seasonal.

For Example: Paddy or wheat production extends only for three or four months a year. But the demand for paddy or wheat is throughout the year.

Different Quality and Quantity

The quality and quantity of agricultural products are beyond the control of the producers. They also very from year to year region village to village and climate to climate. The weather is not under the control of human being and greatly affects the quality and quantity of produce. They are also affected due to flood, drought, plant diseases, and ubsects.

Perishability

Many agricultural goods are perishable by nature perishable products like fruits, vegetables, milk, dairy products poultry products, meat etc. These perishable products need cold storage facility.

Consumption Characteristics

Inelastic Demand and Supply

Agricultural goods are necessary for every human being hence their demand is also inelastic. Price changes do not effect the demand. Demand for food-grains is not affected by fall or rise in price. Price fluctuates due to imbalance in supply and demand. Government takes necessary steps to stabilise price in order to protect the countless small farmers form adverse price changes, Government purchase marketed surplus and release as and when needed. Agricultural goods are consumed regularly and in small quantities.

Problems in the Marketing of Agricultural Goods in International Markrt

1. There is high demand for transportation and storage facilities in the harvest seasons in order to protect the produce from deterioration in quality. So special transportation and storage facilities have to be provided.
2. There is a seasonal production so more finance is necessary in a particular period.
3. Grading and standardisation is very important for agricultural products. But it is very difficult to grade

and standardise the products as they are many agricultural goods.

4. There is price fluctuation in agricultural goods due to the imbalance in supply and demand.
5. Production of agricultural products is seasonal. The consumption is regular and the demand is regular through out the year hence commodities must be stored and made available to the consumers.

Review Questions

1. Define marketing of services and its characteristics.
2. What are the kinds of services?
3. Explain different kinds of goods.
4. What are the problems in marketing of agriculture goods in international market?

8 GLOBAL MARKETING RESEARCH

Meaning

Marketing research is simply a scientific search for knowledge especially in the areas related to function of marketing. Marketing research as separate department can be a sources of great help to management decision making.

Research in marketing refers to "The systematic gathering, recording and analysing of data about problems relating to the market of goods and services/as such. The function involved are (i) systematic collection of data and information. (ii) Properly recording them for use and (iii) Analysing and interpreting the recorded facts and figures to arrive at useful conclusion.

Definition

"According to Cundiff and Still".

"Marketing research is a systematic gathering, recording and analysing the data about marketing problem to facilitate decision-making.

Global Marketing Research Process

We have seen in detail the major areas of marketing research in the previous chapter. In this chapter, we are going to study the various steps involved in the marketing research process.

Generally, effective marketing research comprises of the following steps;

1. Problem definition;
2. Research design;
3. Field work or data collection;
4. Data analysis; and
5. Report preparation.

Marketing research provides information to marketing executives and so, marketing decisions are based on information.

Problem Definition

The first step in the research methodology is the definition of the problem to be studied. The objects of the study must be clearly determined beforehand. The statement of research objectives should be limited to a small number of hypotheses to test of questions to answer. The number must be small because no project can produce timely and reliable information for managerial decision if it is directed towards obtaining too many facts.

Hence problem identification and setting the objectives of the study are the two facets of the first step.

Research Design

A research design is a master plan or model for the conduct of formal investigation. The design of the research could be drafted only after making an informal or preliminary investigation into the problem chosen. The investigator can meet consumers, retailers, marketing executives and competitors to collect the required background information. The marketing researcher faces a choice among many ways to collect the information that will fulfill research objectives. He must decide on.

1. Method of data collection; (primary data, Secondary data),
2. Tools to be employed;
3. Sampling design.

When the data needed already exist in an accessible form, this is called secondary data. When satisfactory secondary data are not available, the researcher must collect primary data from customers, middlemen, salesman, competitors or other information sources. Observation technique, experimentation technique and survey method are basic methods of collection of primary data. The observational method makes use of tools like tape-recorders, cameras etc. The survey method and the experimental method commonly use questionnaires. The third element of research design is a sampling plan or sampling design. By employing the sampling technique the sampling plan has to be framed in order to find out answers to the following questions.

1. Who is to be surveyed? (Sampling unit)
2. How many are to be surveyed? (Sampling size)
3. How are they to be selected? (Sampling procedure)
4. How are they to be reached? (Sampling media)

Field Work or Data Collection

After the research design has been formulated the market researcher must undertake the task of data collection or fieldwork. This stage is generally the most expensive and the most liable to error. The following are the major problems faced by the researcher at this stage.

Problems faced by the Researcher at this Stage

Not at Home

When an interview does not find the respondent at home, he can either call back later or substitute the next household. The substitution may introduce bias.

Refusal to Co-operate

The researcher must interact those respondents who refuse to co-operate due to inconvenient time or due to some other reason.

Respondent Bias

In order to finish quickly, the respondents may tend to provide in accurate data and hence, it is the duty of the researcher to encourage and extract accurate answers.

Interviewer Bias

The dishonesty of the interviewer may also make the data biased one. Interviewers face a great temptation to fill their quota of interviewers as quickly as possible.

Data Analysis

In order to extract meaningful information from the data, collected data must be edited, tabulated and analyzed. In order to find out the underlying magnitudes and patterns of association or casualty, various statistical and mathematical tools can be employed. Averages, measures of dispersion, correlation co-efficient and multivariate analysis are commonly used techniques for the data analysis. Electronic Data Processing equipment can also be employed for analyzing large data quickly and at a low cost. Conclusions and interpretations lead to recommendation for action.

Report Preparation

The last step is the preparation of the report incorporating the major findings and recommendation coming from the study. The report must clearly point out the relationship among the data, the interpretation and the recommendations. The report contains the following:

Report Contains

(1) Title page;

(2) Table of contents;

(3) A concise statement of the marketing research problem;

(4) The aims and objectives of the research;

(5) An outline of the research design describing the methodology used;

(6) Limitations of the study;

(7) Data Analysis and its result;

(8) Findings, conclusions and recommendations: and

(9) Appendixes comprising of questionnaire copy, sample design, lengthy tables etc.

In general the report should be written to facilitate the understanding and interest of the marketing executives and their capacity to extract actionable information. Further, the report presented to the management must be followed up to ensure the implementation of the recommendations.

Having seen be the various steps involved in the marketing research methodology, we will discuss some of the important steps in an elaborate way, in the remaining part of this lesson.

Sampling Desing

A research may be conducted by either of the two methods. (1) Census method or (2) Sampling method. When the whole area or population of persons is contacted, the method is known as census method. On the other hand when a small group is selected as representative of the whole mass it is known as sampling method. The expensive nature of census makes it prohibitive to undertake such a study. The time, money and men required for the purpose is so awfully large that it does not seem a practical proposition to undertake such a study, unless it is absolutely correct results with such less time, money and materials. Therefore sampling method is commonly employed technique in the majority of research works and surveys.

When a small group is taken as the representative of the whole universe or population, the study is called as sampling study and the group actually selected for study is known as sample. The person who is most likely to supply the required information will be our respondent or unit in the sample. The person may be a house wife, the husband , family, or the retailer, or a newspaper and so on. The units included in the sample can be easily approached to obtain the desired information for taking marketing decisions.

Data obtained through sampling may contain fewer errors than data gathered through a complete census. For instance, when the universe size is very large and sample selection methods are used, there is a strong possibility that sampling will result in fewer errors. Therefore, when the greater degree of accuracy is desired, the sample size should be enlarged. Since, sample is a study of a part of the population, considerable time and lab our are saving of time and money, it is possible to correct more detailed information.

But at the same time, a sample survey must be carefully planned and executed. Otherwise the results obtained may be inaccurate and misleading. Therefore, sampling generally requires the services of experts.

Sampling designs can be grouped under two broad heads-viz.

Random Sampling Methods

(a) Simple or unrestricted random sampling; and

(b) Restricted random sampling;

  (i) Stratified sampling;

  (ii) Systematic sampling; and

  (iii) Cluster sampling.

Non- Random Sampling Methods

(i) Judgment sampling;

(ii) Convenience sampling; and

(iii) Quota sampling.

The students can learn about these sampling methods in an elaborate way from any standard textbook on "Statistics".

Data Collection

Types of Data

Market researches can gather data from two sources viz.

(i) Internal sources; and

(ii) External sources.

Facts and figures are considered as raw materials for researchers. Internal sources are the firms' own records, account books, documents registers etc. All others sources of information are external sources.

On the basis of the nature of data, data could be classified as:

(i) Secondary data; and

(ii) Primary data is on which is obtained by researcher from original sources.

Secondary data, which is readily available, is compiled by some other agency for some other purposes. Using secondary data is definitely a time and money saving method. But it way have bias since it has been compiled for some other purposes. (1) Government publications, (2) Market Survey Reports, (3) Libraries, (4) Universities, (5) Newspapers, Journals and Trade Journals, (6) Chamber of Commerce and Trade Association, (7) Advertising Agencies, (8) Stock Exchange and Commodity Exchanges and (9) Banks, are some of the sources of secondary data. On the other hand, primary data is one, obtained from the original sources by the researcher, for men and original sales records are primary data. Primary data ensures accuracy and reliability though it could be gathered slowly at a high cost. Further, secondary data may be related to the past period and hence it has a limited utility. But the primary data gives the latest information. Secondary data, which has been collected for a different purpose and available in a particular form may not be suitable to the special requirement of the current marketing research investigation. But primary data is collected for meeting the specific research objectives of the current projects and hence there is no problem of adjustments of the data.

Techniques of Data Collection

When satisfactory secondary data are not available, the marketing researcher must collect primary data. The data can be collected from customers, middlemen, salesmen, competitors and other information sources. There are three basic primary data collection methods.

They are:

1. Observation Technique;
2. Experimentation Technique; and
3. Survey method.

Observation Technique

Under this method marketing research data are collected not through asking any questions, but by observing, and recording.

(a) Sales Technique;

(b) Customer movement;

(c) Customer responses;

(d) Stock audit in retail stores for brands bought;

(e) Poster research, counting cars and people passing by a poster; and

(f) Fashions and style acceptance.

The main advantage of these methods is that it records respondents' expressed actions and behaviors patterns. But this method cannot give information on the state of mind, buying motives and on peoples' account of how they behave.

Experimentation Technique

Experimental method has been universally acclaimed as the most scientific method. This method is considered as an important tool to find out the casual relationship (e.g., effect of price change upon sales, effect of advertising upon sales etc.) The experimental; method consists of introducing selected stimuli into a controlled environment and systematically varying them. To the extent that extraneous factors are eliminated or controlled, the observed effects can be related to the variations in the stimuli. For example, a manufactures wants to know the effect of price change upon the sales.

1. Sample markets are selected;
2. One market will act as control market; Where price remains the same;

3. Prices are changed in other markets;
4. Sales figures are carefully recorded; and
5. Finally, the effect of price changes and sales can be evaluated with reference to sales in the control market where price is not changed.

In the second example, an advertiser, in orders determine the most effective advertisement in one or market areas, may publish two different versions of a proposed advertisement (Advertisement X and Advertisement Y) in a newspaper, with half of the copies of the issue carrying 'advertisement X' and the other half advertisement Y' Experimental method can be applied in finding the

(a) best sales- training method;
(b) the best incentive scheme;
(c) the best price level; and
(d) the best advertisement campaign.

Experimental method permits the determination of cause and effect relationship more clearly than other methods. Though it yields a more precise and accurate results, it is complex, expensive and to administer.

Survey Method

A third method of gathering primary data is through surveys. Survey methods yields a broader range of information when compared with either observation technique or experimentation technique. Surveys can gather information on socio- economic characteristic, attitudes, opinions, motives and over behavior. Surveys are an effective way of gathering information for planning product features advertising media sales promotions, channels of distribution etc.

In this method, information is obtained from individual respondents through the following ways;

(a) Personal interviews;
(b) Mailed questionnaires;
(c) Telephone interviews; and
(d) Panel method.

Personal Interviews

It is the direct form of inquiry involving face-to-face communication. Under this method, the researcher is interested in the objective data secured from the respondent such as income, number of children, standard of living etc., and also in the personality of the informant his irritate, prejudices, likes and dislikes are revealed by his verbal behavior including the subtle gestures that accompany it, such as facial; expression, tone of voice and so on. In personal interviews, both structured and unstructured questions are possible. Complex questions can also be asked. Further, the rate of refusal is also low. Visual aids like pictures, exhibits and advertisements can also be used to get views, opinions and attitudes of respondents. For example the opinion of consumers about the package pattern of product could be gathered through direct inquiries.

Mailed Questionnaire

The mail survey method is a very effective and neat method of collecting data from the respondents. In this method a questionnaire is prepared and then sent by post to the respondents, with a covering letter and stamped reply envelope. The covering letter must be drafted in such a way as to create interest and motivate the respondent to send prompt and accurate replies. The mailed questionnaires method has no geographic limitation. But the response may not be encouraging and the questionnaire may not be completely answered. The construction of a good questionnaire requires a considerable skill. Each question should be checked to determine whether it is necessary in terms of the research objectives.

Examples

1. How do you feel about the styling of this new pressure cooker?

   Excellent –

   Good –

   Fair –

   Poor –

2. What brand of cigarettes do you smoke?
3. Where do you buy most of your groceries?
4. What is your opinion regarding the recent hike in the price per copy of the newspaper...?
5. Why do you use 'Liril Soap'?
6. What feature of the new 'Promise' toothpaste appeals to you most?

Telephone Interviews

In big cities, the marketers can interview people through telephone interviewing stands out as the best method for gathering information quickly. The drawbacks of the telephone interview method are the following:

Drawbacks

1. Only people with telephones can be interviewed;
2. Short interviews can only out; and
3. On the phone people give non-committed answers also.

Panel Method

Under this method, the marketing researcher interviews the same sample group of respondents repeatedly after a time gap to observe the changes in their attitudes and behaviors. Respondents may be individual consumers, retailers, wholesalers, etc. Panels are made up of respondents who keep a diary of purchases, advertising responses and similar and report their buying behavior routinely. Consumer panels are widely used in marketing research to test and evaluate new products, new packages etc. A sample of family units constitute a 'consumer panel' which maintains a dairy of their shopping behavior and reports on a weekly or monthly basis. Consumer panel offers three main advantages to the firm.

1. Buyer behaviour can be related to buyer characteristics;
2. Changes in buyer behaviour can be related to changes in the marketing mix; and
3. Changes in buyer behaviour can be monitored over time.

Review Questions

1. How will you draft a Research Report? What are its contents?
2. Explain the various non-random sampling methods.
3. Distinguish between primary data and secondary data with suitable examples.
4. Explain the meaning and merits of panel method of interviewing the sample group.
5. Explain briefly the various steps in marketing research.
6. What is 'primary data'? Briefly analyses a few methods of collection of primary data.
7. Distinguish between:
   (a) Primary data and Secondary data;
   (b) Mail Survey and Personal Interview; and
   (c) Experimental Technique and observation technique.
8. Consider you are a manufacturer of detergent soap of medium variety and would like to undertake marketing research. Draft the plan for your research programmer.
9. What are the merits of 'Mailed–Questionnaire' method of collecting primary data?
10. What is meant by 'Sampling method'? How will you determine the 'sample' for your survey?

9 GLOBAL MARKETING AUDIT

Definition

"Marketing audit is defined as a systematic, critical and unbiased appraisal of the organisation, methods, procedures and personnel employed to achieve those objectives and implement these polices".

–Edward W. Cundiff and et al,

"A true marketing audit is a systematic and comprehensive appraisal of a company's total marketing operation."

–E.J. Kelley.

It is one of the tools applied by a company for evaluating overall marketing strategy, and finding out whether effectiveness of desired output corresponding to the input is improved or at least maintained.

Basic Characteristics of Global Marketing Audit

A marketing audit has the following four characteristics:

It is Comprehensive

It should cover the following aspects of marketing, i.e., marketing environment, objectives; strategies organisation and systems. The real source of the company's marketing problems can be effectively located by a marketing audit.

It is Systematic

A marketing audit follows an orderly sequence of diagnostic steps analysing the company's marketing environment, internal marketing system and specific marketing activities. After making such an in depth study, it frames as corrective action plan for improving the overall marketing effectiveness of the company.

It Possesses Objectivity and Independence

It is conducted under six methods:

(a) Self audit–When the company uses a check list for rating their own marketing operations.

(b) Audit from across.

(c) Audit from above.

(d) Company auditing office.

(e) Company task-force audit.

(f) Outsider audit.

Above all the methods, the 'outsider audit' is recommended since other methods lack objectivity and independence.

It is Periodically Conducted

If it is to really serve the organisation, it should be conduced periodically. There is no use of reporting to it when the company has become sick, the morale of sales force has fallen, and volume of sale has turned down sharply or in any critical situation.

If it is conducted periodically it will be of great benefit both to prosperous as well as poor companies.

All these characteristics have been included in the following definition given by Philip Kotler:

"A marketing audit is a comprehensive, systematic, independent and periodic examination of company's–or business unit's marketing environment, objectives, strategies and activities with a view of determining problem areas and opportunities and recommending a plan of action to improve the company's marketing performance".

Main Aspects of Marketing Operation Covered by Global Marketing Audit

The following are the main aspects to be covered by marketing audit.

Objectives of Each Input

Objectives of each marketing input should be clearly, Stated in terms of specific desired outputs.

Consistency of Policies

The policies of the company should be appraised as their consistency in achieving the marketing objectives.

Capacity of the Organisation

It should be studied whether the company possesses necessary skill and facilities and planning and control systems to achieve the marketing objectives.

Effectiveness of Strategies

It should study the effectiveness of strategies adopted to carry out the policies.

Design of Procedures

It studies whether steps adopted are logical, well designed and suit the situation.

Evaluation of Personnel

Planning and implementation of marketing programmers are to be evaluated in terms of their effectiveness relating to various marketing operations:

Review Questions

1. Define international marketing audit and its objectives.
2. Explain market auditing process.
3. Discuss different tools used in marketing audit.

10 Export Procedures, Documents, Finance And Promotion

Introduction

Exports form the vital component of foreign trade. Students studying international Trade', should have some basic knowledge of export procedures and also the documents required for this. In this chapter, we shall study briefly about the export procedures and the documents required in this process. Besides, we will also study about the finance required for carrying out of the foreign trade activities; the organisations extending financial support and the role of "Export Credit Guarantee Corporation of India Limited" (ECGC) and also about export promotion.

Export Procedure

Exporting involves lot of formalities and procedures and it is a lengthy and complicated process. First of all, an export is required to register his business with various government agencies. The Government of India has introduced a compulsory pre-shipment inspection of certain selected goods to ensure that high quality standards are maintained. Relevant documents have to be ensuring that high quality standards are maintained. Relevant documents have to be prepared or obtained before shipment post-shipment procedure involves a number of steps which include dispatch of documents by C&F agents to the exporter, shipment advice to importer, presentation of documents to banks, relation of export proceeds and following up of export sales. We shall discuss in greater detail about the various procedures and formalities.

Registration

Unlike domestic busyness, an export is required to get his business registered with various government agencies. The following are some of the main steps:

(a) To decide the nature of business: Exporters generally start their business on a small-scale like sole proprietorship or partnership. This is because; there is lot of uncertainty in export business. When the scale of operation is enhanced, there should be more of inputs and the business can be made as private limited company or joint–stock company, depending upon the size and scale of operation.

(b) To open a bank account: The exporter should open a bank account; and in this, he should be very careful in selecting the bank. He should open a current account in such a bank which would support him in business. As far as possible, he should open as account in a bank which is authorized to deal in foreign exchange. The export must maintain cordial support to the exporter.

(c) To fix Credit limit: The exporter must apply to the bank and get pre-shipment and post-shipment credit limit fixed. This will enable exporter to know much capital he should raise from order sources and the value of orders he should entertain.

(d)To obtain Fax facility: Communication through FAX has become very common in modern days it is also very popular. It is the latest means of communication. In case of established exports, they can own FAX facility; but a new comer can obtain the facility provided by FAX agents.

(e) To obtain Income-Tax Number: The exporter must possess income-tax number from income-tax authorities. A new comer in export business can get a temporary number from income-tax authorizes; later on, when he is settled in business, he can get permanent number.

(f) To obtain Code Number: Every export is required to obtain a Code Number from the Reserve Bank of India. The export

must quote income-tax number allotted to him by the income-tax authorizes on the CNX from which is used for obtaining code number. The exporter must collect two copies of code number application form from the Exchange Control Department (Exports) of RBI. In a sealed envelope, the exporter is required to put two copies of CNX form, a copy of income-tax number certificate and a confidential report about the financial standing from the bank and forward it to RBI. As per the EXIM POLICY (1992-1997), exporters are required to obtain Import-Export code (IEC) number. The exporter is required to apply to the Chief Controller of exports any time of non-prohibited goods. This code number is made compulsory now. It is not applicable for export of services like consultancy or construction contracts.

(g) To register with ECGC: Export Credit and Guarantee corporation which is a division of Ministry of Commerce Provides credit insurance to exporters against commercial and political risks involved, while collecting payments from abroad. The ECGC policy helps to overcome the non-payment risks from the foreign buyers. A policy with ECGC also helps to get liberal credit from the bank. This is because; ECGC gives various kinds of pre-shipment and post-shipment financial guarantees to the bank on behalf of the exporter.

(h) To apply for exemption from sales Tax: The goods meant for exports are eligible for exemption from both State and Central Sales Taxes. The export firm should be registered with sales tax authorized and follow the necessary procedure laid down by them.

(i) To register with Export Promotion Council: There are different exports promotion councils for different types of business like Engineering Export Promotion Council, Chemical Export Promotion Council, Textile Export Promotion Council, etc. the firm should have registration cum membership certificate. A registered exporter becomes eligible to get export incentives and benefits offered by the Ministry of Commerce. Further the export-promotion council it will guide the export with plenty of market information.

(j) To become member of Chamber of Commerce, Productivity Council and Indian Institute of Foreign Trade(IIFT): The exports must take up the membership of local chamber of commerce, productivity council and other trade promotion organisations like IIFT in order to avail the services rendered by these organisations and benefits thereby. The IIFT is an autonomous body which conducts short-term residential training programmed for exports. When the business is well established, it is advisable to take membership in IIFT.

Quotation and Indent

After registration the exports gives a quotation or an offer for sale to the foreign buyer. It is usually in the form of preformed Invoice. This gives information regarding (i) Name and address of the buyer or Consignee; (ii) Description of goods to be sold; (iii) Price; (iv) condition of sale; and (v) other provision such as delivery schedules, payment terms, escalation clause due to rising prices/costs, etc.

In the export trade, it is essential to have a clear understanding as to where the responsibilities of the seller end. The seller would like to quote his price 'ex-works' in his own currency and leave the rest to the foreign purchaser. On the other hand, the buyer or the importer would always prefer to have the goods delivered to his own warehouse free of all charges, at an exclusive price quoted in his own currency. The first type of price quotation is called 'ex-factory' or 'loco' while the second type is called 'Franco' quotation. In a competitive world, the export must go as far as he can to meet the importer's wishes.

The quotation is an offer of sale made by the seller to the buyer and it must include in a clear-cut manner all terms and conditions on which the goods are offered for sale. These relate to quantity, quality, prices terms of delivery discounts, payments etc.

The exporter, at first receives the order or indent from the importer or his agent. The indent contains all important particulars of the transaction such as description and price of goods, instructions for packing making insurance mode of payment to be adopted by exporter, methods or time of delivery of goods details of import license, etc.

When a Performa invoice accepted by the buyer, it becomes a confirmed order and it is a signal for the exporter to precede with the formalities connected with the export of the goods mentioned.

Shipping and Credit Enquiry

Then the exporter may have to arrange for booking of shipping space in advance of actual sending of goods. Usually the exporter hands over this responsibility to a shipping and freight broker who is specialized in this work. He possesses full knowledge of the various shipping lines and gives expert advice as to which line is cheaper.

The shipping company issues a shipping order to the export when it graces to carry the exports goods. The shipping order is a document containing instructions to the Captain of the ship to accept goods on board the ship from the export or hid agent. Then the creditworthiness of the importer should be thoroughly verified. He may be requested to open an account in the form of *letter of credit with a bank having branches in both exporting and importing countries.*

Preparation for Export

In case an export commission house is acting as an agent of the importer, it will be in charge of collection of goods as per indent from exports, i,e., local producers and manufacturers. The indent house will act as a principal in placing orders and securing the supplies as per instructions of the export commission house will have to look after packing and marking of goods as per usage or as per special instructions of importer. If exporter is also a manufacturer, the indent or order is sent to the factory with all specifications and the deadlines for delivery.

(a)Arrangement for Shipment: The manufacture exporter, or merchant exporter can exemption from the sales tax and refund of excise duty and customs duty. Certain legal formalities have to be performed before the goods are released for shipment.

'From 14' is required for exemption of sales tax, and 'Form AR-4' is needed for exemption or refund of excise duty.

(b) Pre-shipment Inspection: We have compulsory quality control for export of goods. Export Inspection Council (EIC) does the pre-shipment inspection. Emphasis is on quality control and not on inspection for export. This is done to prevent export of inferior quality goods which would bring bad name for the country.

Under the Export Inspection Council, effective controls are exercised during the procurement of materials and components and process of production in case of come of the 'panel' items. The ECI relies on rigorous periodical checks of the factory's own system of process control through a panel of experts. The units approved by the panel are declared as "Export Worthy" Exports of such units are allowed without much formality. It is, thus, advisable for manufacturers to get themselves recognized as "export worthy" units.

Procedure for Recognition as Export Worthy Units

(i) The manufacturer has to intimate the nearest Export Inspection Agency for necessary recognitions, which full of quality control measures adopted with regards to his products.

(ii) After preliminary examination of the details furnished, a questionnaire is supplied by the ELA to the unit.

(iii) One receipt of questionnaire duly filled in, a preliminary inspection by a panel of Experts if fixed.

(iv) On satisfactory report in a prescribed manner by the 'Panel', the unit is declare "export worthy" or "not export worthy".

For inspection of export goods, two different systems are to be followed; one in respect of panel items and the other for Non-Panel. Panel items are those goods which come from "Export Worthy" units for purpose of export, and as such, pre-shipment inspection for them will be a mere formality by making intimation by the export to EIA. In the case of *Non-Panel items*, compulsory inspection prior to shipment is carried out. For this the exporter should apply in the prescribed from to EIA concerned, before the expected date of shipment with the following documents: (i) Copy of commercial invoice; (ii) A crossed cheque or demand draft for necessary fee in favor of EAI; (iii) Copy of export contract; (iv) Deceleration regarding importers technical specifications of quality in support of the deceleration of this specifications. Inspection is generally carried out in rest of a specified percentage of the lot on the basis of ELA's scales of sampling. It also includes examination of the packing on consignment and packing material for its quality, design and ability to withstand damage and the entire consignment marked and sealed with official EIC Seal under its personal supervisor. Incase of rejection copy of rejection Note' is sent with an appeal to the EIA to convene a meeting of the Panel Experts. They review the inspection report, here the export if necessary and even examine the consignment concerned. Their report is finalized within there days and is binding on the parties, the EIA and the exporter.

(c) Forwarding Agent: In order to take after all shipping and customs formulates and the actual loading of the goods on board the ship, a specialist called Forwarding Agent may be appointed by the exporters. These forwarding agents are expert in their line of business and on normal commission offer valuable services to exporter. In particular, they perform the following functions: (i) Negotiations of shipping contract; (ii) Customs formalities; (iii) Marine insurance; and (iv) Loading of goods and securing Bill of Lading. Sometimes the forward agents may be entrusted with the work of packing marking, etc., of the goods to be exported.

(d) Packing: Packing may be done either by the manufacturer himself or in may be entrusted to 'Packing Agents'. Packing for export is highly specified work. Firstly, placing must to only provide adequate protection for the goods and of the customs authorizes. Secondly the goods may perhaps refuse to take devilry. The forwarding agents are experienced in the general routine of exports to packing etc.

(e) Marking: Each packing should be stamped with a distinct mark pointing out the name of the importer and port of

destination. The gross weight, weight with package and the weight along with measurements should be marked on the package.

Customers and Exchange Formalities

The necessary sets to be undertaken under this are as follows:

(a) Shipping Bills: The shipping bill or custom challan contains detailed description of the goods, viz, quality quantity, value, numbers, marks, measurement, the port of destination, the name of the ship carrying the goods etc. the exporter is required to fill in there copies of shipping bills.

(b) Export Permission Forms: it is an application to export. This application form should be filled in duplicate and the exporter submits four copies of shipping bill and two copies of application to exporter to the landing and shipping dues office. This office collects shipping dues or charges, retains one copy of application and returns to the exporter the other along with there copies of shipping bills.

(c) Customers House: The exporter is required to present a copy of application, three copies of shipping bill, and export license (for verification) to the customs house. Shipping bills for dutiable goods differ from those for free goods. The customs house will register details of export with necessary endorsement. The original and duplicate copy of the shipping bill is retained by the customs house. Export duty, if any, will have to be paid. The customs house will direct the examining officer or reference to value description, quality etc. a custom export pass will be issued in favor to the satisfaction of the customs house.

(d) Export License: At present, every exporter is required to procure export license from the controller of exports for those commodities for which license are required. It is valid for there months, though the period can be extended by licensing authority.

(e) Exchange control: Formality, when the foreign Exchange Regulation Act (FERA) was in force, the procedures were stringent and taxing. With the introduction of foreign Exchange Management Act (FEMA), the procedures were very much simplified.

The exporter has to fill in four GR Forms. One copy would be given to the customers house at the time of shipment and three copies of GR Forms should be given to the authorized exchange declare along with one copy of invoice and other shipping documents. The exchange dealer. The foreign exchange bank, will forward two copies of GR Forms to the reserve Bank of India.

Mate's Receipt

After having received back the two copies of shipping bill and one copy of the application to Exporter the shipper makes arrangements to place the goods on board the ship. He has to hand over one copy of the shipping bill at the dock while the goods are taken in. The Captain of the ship or the Mate who is his assistant cannot allow the shipping of the goods, unless the shipper presents to either of them a copy of the shipping bill and counting of the packages. This receipt is called the 'Mate's Receipt'. If the Mate is not satisfied with packing of the goods, a remark to that effect is made on the receipt. A receipt with this remark thereon is regarded as a clean Mate's Receipt. This remark is transferred to the Bill of Lading when the exporter gets it in exchange for the Mate's Receipt.

Insurance

While the work connected with the shipping of the goods is being carried out, the exporter makes arrangements with some Marine Insurance company for insurance the goods to safeguard them against marine risks. Usually, the goods are insured for the amount which covers not only the value of the goods, but also a reasonable profit (generally 15 percent of the value of the goods) and reasonable expenses expected to be incurred in the event of the loss or destruction of the goods by the perils of the sea.

Bill of Lading

The exporter approaches the shipping Company, presents the Mate' Recipe and in exchange receives a documents known as bill of lading. Actually, the exporter himself fills in the details regarding the goods, destination, name of the ship, etc. The authorized person, on behalf of the shipping Company, checks, signs and return this Bill of Lading to the export along with the freight note, as soon as the freight charges are also paid by the exporter. Freight Note is, thus, a receipt of having paid the requisite freight to the shipping company by the shipper.

Sometimes the importer agrees to pay the freight according to the contract between the exporter and importer. In such a case, the exporter gets the Bill of Lading duly signed and stamped by the Shipping Company and marked with the words 'Freight Forward'. When the goods in such a case reach the importer's destination, he presents the bill of Lading along with the payment of the freight and then only the importer can take charge of the goods. A Bill of Lading may be defined as a document wherein the steamship company gives its official receipts for goods shipped in one of its vessels and at the same time contracts to carry to the part of destination.

The possession of this document, i.e., Bill of Lading gives the title, i.e., the partnership to the goods and it is freely transferred by endorsement and delivery. The export sends this bill of lading to the importer who can take possession of the goods by presenting the same to the shipping company at his station port. The Bill of Lading is said to be 'clean' if it is signed without any adverse remarks on it. A clean Bill of Lading is an evidence of the goods having been packed in good condition at the time of loading.

Other Shipping Documents

(a) Letter of Industry: If the Bill of Lading contains some adverse remarks regarding packing of the goods, the importer may refuse to talk delivery or may claim damage. In order to avoid this trouble, the exporter gives to the shipping company a Latter of Indemnity by which he agrees to indemnify the shipping company, in return for a clean Bill of Lading for any claim on the part of the importer in respect of the goods.

(b) Consular Invoice: In those countries where advalorem duties are charged, it is in the interest of the importer to present to the customs authorities charged of the importing country the document called 'Consular Invoice' in order to save time and trouble while taking delivery of the goods. This invoice has to be sent him by the exporter who fills in a special form and gets certified by the consulate of the importing country stationed in the exporting country.

The customs authorized of the importing country considered this invoice as a genuine statement of the contents and value of the goods. This document thus rids the importer of the trouble of opening all the packages at the time of assessing the duties by the customs house.

(c) Certificate of Origin: Trade Agreements between two countries may offer a differential treatment in respect of import duties to the goods sent from one country to other, 'the most favored nation' treatment, as it is often called. In these cases, the importer will get some advantage in import duties, as the goods have been purchased from the favored nation. As per trade agreement. In order to that the import goods originated from the export company with whom the trade agreement has been entered into, the importer has to present to Customs authorities the certificate called,' Certificate of Origin'. This document exporter of goods will obtain this certificate from the chamber of commerce and send it to the importer to make use of it.

Securing Payment

The exporter can resort to a number of alternatives for securing payment of export dues from the importer. This depends on his contact with the importer.

Export Finance

We shall study about export finance. Finance is an essential requirement for any kind of business. So is the case with exporter. The various resources available have to be explored in order to fulfill the finance requirements of the exporter. We can define exporter finance as "the credits required by exporters for financing their exporter transactions from the time of getting an export order to the time of the full realizations from the time of getting an export order to the time of the full realization of the payment from the importers."

From the time of an export order is received and confirmed, the exporter needs finance at pre-shipment stage and also at post-shipment stage. Finance is required at pre-shipment stage for the following purpose (a) To purchase raw materials and other inputs to manufacture goods; (b) To assemble the goods in the case of merchant exporters; (c) To store the goods in suitable warehouses till the goods are shipped; (d) To pay for packing, marking and labeling of goods; (e) To pay for pre-shipment inspection charges; (f) To pay for consultancy services; (g) To import or purchase from the domestic market heavy machinery and other capital goods to produce export goods; and (h) To pay for export documentation expenses.

Finance is needed at the *post-shipment* stage for the following:

(a) To pay to agents/distributors and others for their services. (b) To pay for publicity and advertising in the overseas markets. (c) To pay for port authorities, customs, and shipping agent's charges. (d)To pay towards export duty or tax, if any. (e) To pay towards ECGC premium. (f) To pay for freight and other shipping expenses. (g) To pay towards marine insurance premium, especially when it is a CIF contract. (h) To pay towards various expenses in connection with visits abroad for market surveys, or for some other purpose. (i) To pay for collecting information on overseas markets either participation in exhibitions and trade fairs in India and abroad. (j) To pay for representatives abroad in connection with their stay abroad. (k)To pay for any other activity in connection with export of goods.

Pre-shipment credit or 'packing Credit': This is advance granted to the exporters by the banks for meeting their such financial requirements as purchase of raw materials and its processing, packing, storing and shipping of goods. It is a short term credit which is available to all exporters. Pre-shipment finance is essentially working capital finance made available to the exporters to arrange for goods as per the export order. It is generally granted in the form of overdraft facilities. The exporter interested in availing the pre-shipment credit facility will have to make formal applications to his bank along with a form contract with the buyer or a copy of the exporter order or a copy of the letter of credit.

Post-shipment Finance: This is provided to meet working capital requirements after the actual shipment of goods. It bridges the financial gap between the date of shipment and actual receipt of payment form overseas buyer thereof. This finance is extended to the actual exporter who has shipped buyer thereof. This finance is extended to the actual exporter who has shipped the goods or to an exporter whose name, export under documents are transferred. It can also be allotted to overseas buyer/institutions under the scheme for for Buyer's Credit and Lines of document operated by EXIM Bank. It is extended against the evidence of shipping documents indicating the actual shipment of goods or necessary evidence in case of deemed exports.

Forms of post-shipment finance may be provided in one of the following forms. (a) Export bills negotiated under LC. (b) Purchase of export bills drawn under confirmed counteracts. (c) Advance against bills under collection (d) Advance against export incentives receivables. (e) Advance against undrawn balance of bills (f) Advance against Deemed exporters.

The amount of post-shipment finance depends upon whether it is short-term, medium-term or long-term. It is also depends upon the value of capital goods and equipment or turnkey projects. Any loan up to Rs. 10 Crores for financing export of capital goods is decided by commercial bank which can refinance itself from EXIM Bank. In case of export contract bank Rs. 10 crores but not more than Rs. 50 crores, the EXIM bank has the authority to decide whether export finance could be provided. Contracts above Rs. 50 crores need the clearance from the working group on Export Finance, consisting of representatives from EXIM Bank, RBI, ECGC and the bankers of the exporter. In case of large contracts, representative from

Ministries of Commerce and finance also act as members of Working Group.

The period of post-shipment finance may be short-term, medium-term or long-term. Short-term is usually 90 days. The loan is provided by commercial bank. Medium-term is usually between 90 days and 5 days, and the commercial bank togerther with EXIM Bank gives medium term loans. The long-term is the period above 5 years to 12 years and it is provided and turnkey projects. The rate of interest for the loan depends upon the directives of the RBI from time to time.

Before disbursement of loan, the bank requires the exporter to executive a formal loan agreement. The post-shipment credit advances are not sanctioned in lump-sum; but disbursed in a phased manner and the bank has the power to monitor the use of the credit by the exporter i.e. whether the amount is used for the export purpose or not, penalty can be imposed for misuse. As per the directive of RBI, the bank must maintain separate account in respect of each post-shipment advace. It is to be noted that this post-shipment loan should be redeemed only from the proceeds of the export and it cannot be done by local funds available with the exporter. In the case, the loan will not be treated as post shipment loan and concessional interest rates will not be granted.

Institutional Support to Export Finance

Generally, major part of export finance is provided by Commercial banks of the country. The commercial banks rendered institutional support to exporters, not only in offering credit for purposes; but also renders some non-fund based services to the exporter to carry on his export activities quite smoothly. Apart from the commercial banks, the RBI has a decisive role in export finance though it does not directly provide finance to the exporters, but adopts policies in such a way as to encourage commercial banks and other financial institutions to provide liberal export finance. The role played by EXIM bank and the ECGC is in no way small inextending institution support for financing export trade. We shall briefly study about all these institutions which support export finance.

Role of Commercial Banks in Export Finance

A major part of export finance is provided by commercial banks. They also provide other services and facilities to the exporters. Hence, the services of commercial banks to the exporters can be grouped under two heads, viz, (i) Fund Based Service; and (ii) Non-Fund Based Service.

(i) Fund Based Service: The Commercial banks provide fund based activities at Pre-shipment stage and also at Post-shipment stage by providing finance for a normal of 180 days at a very concessional rate of interest. The various forms of advantages are: (a) Cash Packing credit loan (b) Advantage against hypothecation (c) Advantage against pledge and (d) Other forms. At the post-shipment stage, the commercial banks provide finance normally for a period of 90 days at a concessional rate of unrest. The various forms of Post-shipment finance are:

(a) Negotiation of Bills drawn under LC (b) Purchase/ Discounting of Bills.

Financial and Fiscal Incentives and Assistant

The Government of India has introduced a series of financial and fiscal measures to encourage exporters and to promote exports. These measures include:

(a) Duty Drawback Scheme
(b) Exemption of Sales Tax
(c) Exemption of Excise Duty
(d) Refund of octroi duty
(e) Exemption of Income–tax
(f) Concessions in Railway and Air freight
(g) Finance at low rates of interest
(h) Marketing Development Assistance
(i) Export Credit Risk Insurance.

Export Marketing Assistance

Apart from providing financial assistances to develop export markets, the Government of India also provides non-financial marketing assistances to promote and market our export goods and services. These measures include:

(a) Market Orientation Tours
(b) Overseas Market Surveys
(c) Trade Fairs and Exhibitions
(d) Bilateral Agreements
(e) Sponsoring Trade Delegations and study-cum-sales teams
(f) Collection and dissemination of market information
(g) Export Packaging Assistance
(h) Training Facilities
(i) Buyer-seller meets, etc.

Export Production Assistance

The exporters are provided with a number of facilities and assistance in respect of production of goods for export purpose. These measures include:

1. IRMAC Scheme
2. Priority in allotment of foreign exchange for the import of Capital goods and equipment.
3. Priority of supply of indigenous or raw materials at international prices.
4. Technical and Managerial Guidance.
5. Quality Control Assistance and Guidelines.
6. Granting of permission for foreign collaboration.
7. Reorientation of industrial licensing and import licensing policy towards export.
8. Relaxation of MRTP Act provisions etc.

Institutional and Infrastructural Measures

The Government of India has established a number of organisations which are entrusted with the promotional efforts in the field of exports. These organisations include:

(a) Export Promotion Councils (EPCs)
(b) Commodity Bards (CBs)
(c) Indian Institute of Foreign Trade (IIFT)
(d) Indian Institute of Packaging (IIP)
(e) Export Inspection Council (EIC)
(f) Export Credit and Guarantee Corporation of India (ECGC)
(g) Export-Import Bank of India (EXIM)
(H) Free Trade Zones/Export Processing Zones (FTZ/EPZ)
(i) Indian Council of Arbitration
(j) Federation of Indian Export Organisations (FIEO) etc.

IRMAC Scheme

The STC, MMTC, Export houses and other similar agencies have Industrial Raw Materials Assistance Centers. Such centers import raw materials and components in bulk and then supply to registered Exporters and Actual users against valid import licenses. Such scheme enables exporters to get timely supply of raw materials at reasonable prices.

Duty Drawback Scheme

Duty Drawback means refund of custom duties paid on the import of raw materials components and packing material. It also involves refund of central excise duties paid on indigenous material used in the manufacture of export products.

Exemption from Excise Duty

Export goods are exempted from Central Excise Duty. There are two systems of excise clearance (i) Export under rebate; and (ii) Export under bond. In the case of export under rebate first duty is paid, then a refund is claimed and in case of export under bond, duty is not paid, but an indemnity bond is executed in favor of excise authorities.

Exception from Income Tax

Income from exports is exempted from the payment of income-tax under section 80 HHC. A five year holiday is provided to 100 per cent EOUs and units in FTZ, EPZs.

Exemption from Sales Tax

Export goods are also exempted from the payment of sales-tax. Necessary documents are to be provided to the sales tax authorities, giving proof of export on order to claim sales tax exemption.

Marketing Development Assistance

Large exporters such as export houses, trading houses, and star trading houses are giving marketing development assistance which between 25 per cent to 60 per cent of the actual expenditure incurred. MDA is provided in respect of conducting market surveys, advertising and publicity abroad, opening show-rooms in India and abroad.

Export promotion Capital Goods Scheme (EPCG)

Under this scheme, import of capital goods is permitted at a concessional import duty of 15 percent subject to export obligation of four times the CIF value of imports, to be achieved over five years.

There are plenty of export promotion measures adopted by the Government of India and the list enumerated above is only partial.

Export Pricing

Lastly, we shall discuss about'. Export pricing involves fixing the price of product or service which the exporter intends to sell in the overseas markets. Export pricing is much more difficult than domestic pricing because the exporter has to take into account, not only the cost of production, but also the influence and impact of the conditions prevailing in the international market. Therefore, export pricing is not just an arithmetical calculation, but a practical proposition, based on market situation. The success of an export firm largely depends on its effective pricing policy.

Objectives of Export Pricing

Survival: The main objective of pricing is survival in the competitive market. An exporter faces competition not only from his fellow-exporters but also from other countries exporters. In such competitive markets, one of the marketing tools which can make the exporter survive in the competition is pricing. Making price competitive, thereby earning less profit in order to survive, could be one of the objectives of pricing. Keeping prices competitive and maintaining low prices is a short- term objectives as every exporter aims increasing profits at a later stage.

Maximum Sales Growth: As an exporter survives the competition the objective shifts to having maximum sales growth. Depending upon competition and sensitivity of market to price, the final decision needs to be taken. There are two alternatives available for this purpose: (a) *Setting prices to overseas* buyers will lead to higher sales volume, thereby earning more profits. For this, market should be highly price-sensitive. Such low prices discourage competition and thereby sales are increased. (b) *Setting higher prices* to indicate superior quality of the products. Such indication leads consumers to rate products higher compared to that of competitors. Due to this perception of the consumers, sales volume of the product will increase.

Maximum Current Profit: An export may determine his objective of securing maximum profits. A price which would generate such a profit is to be established. For this purpose, it is necessary to have complete information of cost and demand. A price which can generate maximum cash flows or higher rate of return is determined. But this objective is a short term nature and at times this objective may turn out to be dangerous in the export markets.

Establishment: Another objective behind pricing is to establish not only a superior quality image, but also emphasis on leadership or number one position in the export markets.

By charging a higher price and making a noticeable difference in the price as compared to that of competitors these objectives can be fulfilled.

Factors Determining Exports Price

Determining export price depends upon several factors. The exporter has to evaluate all these factors before arriving at a conclusion in determining the price of the commodity to be sold in the international market. The exporter cannot be led purely by the arithmetic of costing. The following factors determine the export pricing decision:

Cost: This is one of the important factors which should be taken into consideration, since costs constitute a large part of the price and the exporter should cover up direct costs such as raw materials and also indirect costs such as distribution overheads.

Demand: Price of goods to a great extent depends upon demand curve. For instance, an increase in demand may lead to an increase in price even though there is no rise in costs.

Competition: The competition in foreign market decides the pricing of export products. The exporter has to compete, not only in the home market, but also in the foreign market. There is much greater possibility of developing countries exports being substituted by products coming from developed countries, if there is price advantage, the price should be reasonably fixed within the range of those competitors.

(a) Overdraft against bills under collection; and (b) Other forms. We have already studied in detail about commercial banks' loans to the exporters at the pre-shipment stage and also at the post-shipment stage.

Non-Fund Based Service

(a) RBI has authorized commercial banks to issue guarantees and furnish bid bonds in favour of overseas buyers. Prior permission of RBI is not required except in case of exports of capital goods under deferred payments, construction contract, consultancy and technical services contract and turnkey projects. Thus, the commercial banks render most valuable service to exporters by performing Guarantee Service in various ways: (b) Performance Guarantee: This is generally required in export of capital goods and also in case of turnkey and construction projects; (c) Guarantee for loans in foreign currency sanctioned by a financial institution abroad to Indian exporters who raise funds in foreign currencies for financing their operations with their projects abroad. (d) The banks also issue advance payment of retention money by the overseas party who normally makes certain advance payment to the Indian exporter against a bank guarantee. (e) Banks also issue guarantee for payment of retention money by the overseas party who would release the retention money to the Indian party, only after receiving guarantee from bank. (f) Bank issue Bid Bonds so as to enable exporters to participate in various global tenders.

Other Services Rendered by Commercial Bank to the Exporter

(a) They collect export proceeds from the importer and credit the same to exporter's account. (b) The banks assist the exporter in the collection of useful information on the credit-worthiness of the foreign buyer through their foreign agents/branches. (c) The banks also provide information on import trade control and exchange control regulations. (d) The banks provide foreign exchange remittance facilities. (e) The banks issue bank drafts in case of payment of freight chargers and such other charges. (f) The banks send the duplicate copy of GR form to the RBI, after realization of export proceeds. (g) The banks also provide information on the exchange rates of various countries. (h) The banks also issue bank certificates, in respect of export sales value which are useful for claiming incentives.

Role of RBI in Export Finance

The Reserve Bank of India, the Central Bank of our country does not directly provide finance to the exporters. But it adopts several policies for initiating measures and encourage commercial banks and other financial institutions to provide liberal credit to exporters. RBI has developed various schemes to encourage commercial banks to provide export to the export sector. The schemes of RBI are: (a) Export Bills Credit Scheme; 1963; (b) Pre-shipment Credit Scheme 1969; (c) Export Credit Interest subsidy Scheme 1968; (d) Refinance under Duty Drawback Credit Scheme 1976.

(a) *Export Bills Credit Scheme:* Under this scheme, RBI used to grant advances to scheduled banks against export bills, maturing within 180 days. Now, this scheme is not in operation.

(b) *Pre-shipment Credit Scheme:* Under this scheme, RBI provides refinance facilities to scheduled banks that provide pre-shipment loans to bonafide exporters.

(c) *Export Credit Interest Subsidy Scheme:* Under this scheme, RBI provides interest subsidy of minimum 1.5 per cent to banks that provide export finance to exporters, provided, the banks charge interest to exporters within the ceiling prescribed by RBI. The subsidy is given both against packing and post-shipment.

(d) *Duty Drawback Credit Scheme:* Under this, the exporters can avail interest free advances from the Bank up to 90 days against shipping bills provisionally certified by customs authorities towards a refund of customs duty. These advances of commercial banks are eligible for refinance from RBI.

Apart from the above mentioned schemes, the Reserve Bank of India also approves or sanctions applications made by the exporters for:

(a) Allotment of Exporters' Code Number, which is a must for every exporter. (b) Extension of time limit for realization of export proceeds, (c) Reduction in invoice price of export goods. (d) Fixation of commission to overseas consignee or agents. (e) Provision of blanket permit where a lump sum exchange is released for a number of purposes. (f) Remittances abroad in respect of advertising, legal expenses, etc. (f) Appointments of foreign nationals as technical and non- non-technical personnel in Indian firms, (h) Appointment of non-residents as directors of Indian companies. (i) Any other matter relating to foreign trade that requires clearance from Exchange Control Department of RBI. (j) Clearance in respect of joint-ventures abroad.

Role of Exim Bank in Export Finance

The Export-Import Bank of India came into existence on January, 1, 1982 and started functioning from March 1, 1982. It has its headquarters in Mumbai and its branches of offices in important cities in India and abroad.

Exim Bank was established for the purpose of financing medium and log term loans to the exporters there by promoting foreign trade in the country. It took over the functions of international wing of IDBI. The main objectives of EXIM Bank are as follows:

(a) Provide financial assistance (medium and long term) to exporters and importers. (b) Functioning as the principal financial institutions for co-coordinating the working of institutions engaged in providing export finance. (c) Promotion of foreign trade of India. (d) To deal with all matters that may be considered to be incidental or conducive to the attainment of above objectives.

Functions of Exim Bank

The services rendered by EXIM Bank to the process can be discussed under two heads, viz., Fund Based Service, and Non-Fund Based Service.

Fund Based Service

Under this, the Exim Bank renders assistance to (i) Indian Exporters; (ii) Overseas Buyers and Agencies; and (iii) Indian Commercial banks.

Assistance to Indian Exporters

(a) Provides direct financial assistance to exporters on deferred payment terms. (b) Finance export and import of machinery and equipment on lease basis. (c) Finances Indian joint ventures in foreign countries. (d) Provides pre-shipment finance to eligible exporters for procuring raw material and other inputs required to produce machinery and equipment to be exported. (e) Offers credit facilities to "Deemed Exports". (f) Provides Computer Software Exporters foreign exchange loan subject to RBI clearance. (g) Provides finance facility against deferred credit to exporters of consultancy, consultancy, technology and other services. (h) Provides finance to Indian exporters to undertake various export marketing activities in India and abroad through Export Marketing Fund (EMF). (i) Operators Exports, Development Fund (EDF) to finance techo-economic survey/research or any other study for the development of Indian Exports.

Assistance to Overseas Buyers and Agencies

(a) EXIM Bank offers 'Overseas Buyer's Credit facility' to foreign importers for import of Indian capital goods and related services with repayment spread over a period of years. (b) Long term finance is also provided under "Lines of Credit" to finance government and financial institutions abroad, which in turn, extend finance to importers of their country to buy Indian capital goods. (c) It provides relending facility to overseas bank to make available term finance to their clients for import of Indian goods.

Assistance to Indian Commercial Banks

(a) EXIM Bank provides refinance facilities so as to enable commercial banks to offer credit to Indian exporters who extend term credit to importers. (b) It offers Export Bills Rediscounting facility to commercial banks in India so that it helps commercial bank to fund-shipment credit extended to Indian exporters.

Non-Fund Based Assistance is divided into two groups:

(i) Financial Guarantees and Bonds.

(ii) Advisory and other Services.

Financial Guarantees and Bonds: EXIM Bank provides non-fund based assistance in the form of guarantees in the nature of bid bonds, performance guarantee etc. These guarantees are provided together with commercial banks. We have discussed already about this.

Advisory and other Services: (a) It advises Indian companies in executing contracts abroad, and on sources of overseas financing. (b) It advises Indian exporters on global exchange control practices. (c) The EXIM Bank offers financial and advisory services to Indian construction project abroad. (d) It advises small-scale manufacturers on export markets and products. (e) It provides access to Euro financing sources and global credit sources to Indian exporters. (f) It assists the exporters under forfeiting scheme.

Forfeiting Scheme

Forfeiting is introduced in Indian recently by the EXIM Band under the approval of RBI. It is popular in other countries. Under this credit system, the exporter gets his export receivables on non-resource discounting basis. Exporters will have to surrender the right of receiving export proceeds to the forfeiters when he receives the discounted amount from him. This is as good as cash sales. There are forfeiting agencies operating in the export field. All exports receivable under deferred payment contract can be forfeited against bills of exchange or promissory note backed by co-acceptance to buyer's bank and endorsed by exporter.

Role of Export Credit Guarantee Corporation of India Limited (ECGC) in Export Finance

In order to provide export credit and insurance support to Indian exporters, the Government of India set up the Export Risks Insurance Corporation (ERIC) in July 1957. It was transformed into Export Credit Guarantee Corporation Limited (ECGC) in 1964. Since 1983, it is known as ECGC of India Ltd. It is a company wholly owned by the Government of India. It functions under the administrative control of the Ministry of Commerce and is managed by a Board of Directors representing Government, Banking, Insurance, Trade and Industry.

The functions of ECGC are mainly helping exporters in obtaining financial assistance from commercial banks and other financial institutions on the strength of its policies and guarantees. It helps in collecting and disseminating information to exporters regarding credit-worthiness of overseas buyers. It also helps in developing and diversifying exports. It insures the exporters credit risks and guarantees payment to the export who can afford credit with confidence and enlarge his overseas business with a sense of security. It charges a low rate of premium to enable the exporters to compete effectively in the overseas market. It provides risk coverage against political and commercial risks. It provides a service which is not available from commercial insurance companies.

Commercial Risks covered by ECGC are as Follows

(i) These risks are of a trade nature which arises out of:

(a) Buyer's failure to accept goods; (b) Buyer's protracted default to pay for goods accepted by him; and (c) Insolvency of the buyer.

Political Risks covered by ECGC are as follows:

(i) These risks arising out of disturbances in political situations of a country such as war, Revolution or Civil disturbances in the country of the producer of goods.

(ii) Imposing new license restrictions or cancellation of valid license in the buyer's country.

(iii) Restrictions on remittance of money in buyer's country.

(iv) Cancellation of export license or imposing of additional licensing restriction preventing the exporter from exporting goods.

(v) Additional handling, transport or insurance charges due to interruption or diversion of voyage which cannot be recovered from the purchaser.

(vi) Imposition of restrictions on remittances by the government in the buyer's country or any government action may block to delay payment to the exporter.

(vii) Any other case of loss occurring outside India, which is not normally covered by commercial insurers and which is beyond either of exporter or importer.

Risks not Covered by ECGC

Exporters should bear in mind that ECGC does not cover the following risks:

(a) General or marine insurance risk which will result in loss, theft, or damage to goods.

(b) Failure of the exporter to fulfil the terms of the export contract, or negligence on his part.

(c) Default or insolvency of any agent of the exporter or of the collecting bank.

(d) Causes inherent in the nature of the goods.

(e) Buyer's failure to obtain exchange authorization from authorities in his country.

(f) Fluctuations in the exchange rate of currency of the invoice.

(g) Commercial disputes raised by the buyer, unless the export obtains a decree from a competent court of law in the buyer's country in his favor.

Various Polices issued by ECGC

The Policies issued by ECGC can be divided broadly into four groups:

(a) *Specific Policies:* These are issued to protect them against risk involved in (i) exports on deferred terms of payment; (ii) Services rendered to foreign parties, and (iii) Construction work and turnkey projects undertaken abroad.

(b) *Standard Policies:* These are issued to exporters to protect them against payment risks involved in exports on short term credit.

(c) *Financial Guarantees:* These are issued to banks in India to protect them from risks of loss involved in their extending financial support, to exporters at pre-shipment and post-shipment stage; and

(d) *Special Schemes:* Transfer Guarantee meant to protect banks which add confirmation to letters of credit opened by foreign banks, insurance cover for Buyer's credit etc.

Thus, the ECGC renders very valuable services in the field of export finance.

Review Questions

1. What is export procedures? Explain in detail.
2. What is export finance? Discuss the role of commercial banks in export finance.
3. What are the factors are considered for export finance?
4. Write the role of RBI in export finance.
5. Explain the role of EXIM bank in export finance.
6. What are the roles of ECGC in export finance?
7. Define export promotion and its procedures.
8. What is export price? Discuss factors of export price.
9. Name the institutions that are involved in export finance.
10. What are the different types of finance available to an export?

11 G.A.T.T., W.T.O., TRIPS AND TRIMS

The foreign trade of a country is powerfully affected by international conflicts and international agreements. Trade policy refers to measures which a country adopts for the purpose of regulating the exchange of goods with other countries in the context of economic development. Tariff, quotas and exchange restrictions indicate the structural contents of a trade policy. Trade Agreements arise from the trade policy of a country. Trade agreements are of two types, viz., Bilateral Agreement and Multilateral Agreement. When a country enters into trade agreement with another country for the sale and purchase of certain specified goods, the agreement is bilateral. Quantity rates and terms of payment are decided in the agreement and it will be for a definite period with provision for extension. Generally, political relations play a very important part in promoting or preventing bilateral trade agreements. A country may have trade agreements with a number of countries for sale and purchase of goods. Such agreements are multilateral and are promoted by international trade organizations or associations.

The maintenance of convertibility of a country's currency is difficult, and therefore, such agreements provide scope for converting export surplus to currencies with which gross deficit can be met.

Imperial Preference and Ottawa Agreement

Towards the end of the 19th century, the British Industrial supremacy was threatened by some of the countries, particularly, Germany and Japan. There was cut-throat competition from these countries in the international market against British goods. Hence, at the beginning of the 20th Century, British Statesmen like Joseph Chamberlin advocated a policy of IMPERIAL PREFERENCE to consolidate the markets within the British Empire for the benefit of British manufactures. The scheme aimed at reducing import duties on goods imported from the countries within the British Empire. In order words, it indicated the imposition of higher import duties on non-Empire goods, and thereby attempted to eliminate competition of the countries outside the British Commonwealth.

This scheme was welcomed by some European countries. Canada took the lead and lowered import duties on some British goods. All the Dominions of the British Empire, because of their subordination to British rule, had to give preference to British foods according to this scheme from 1905 to 1914. The government of India accepted the scheme of imperial preference only in small measure and reduced the export duty in hides and skins sent to Britain, whereas the duty was kept at a higher level in the exports to other countries. The Government did not agree with the scheme is full, as India did not stand to gain from Imperial Preferences. The real fact was that most of the Indian exports, like agricultural products, raw materials, spice and tea, were in great demand all over the world that Indian goods were not in need of any preference. Further, the Indian Government feared that retaliatory measures would be taken up by non-empire countries against Indian goods by levying heavy import duties in their countries. Moreover, giving preference to British goods in India meant competition against Indian goods and obstruction to rising industry in India. Thus, the scheme was not suited to Indian economic interests.

But, the situation changed after some years. The world-wide depression in the thirties affected India's foreign trade severely and Indian exports declined heavily. The economy was passing through a crisis. In such a condition, India was willing to join the scheme of Imperial Preference, as any measure to help India's trade was solicited. A conference was held in Ottawa, Canada, in 1932 and the scheme of Imperial preference was agreed upon. India was also one of the signatories of the Ottawa Agreement.

According to the Ottawa Agreement, British agreed to give free entry to Indian cotton and jute manufactures, hides and skins, vegetables oils, rice, groundnut, coffee, tea, tobacco, teak, etc. in return, India promised to grant a 7.5 per cent preference to British automobiles, a 10 per cent preference to cotton textiles, iron and steel goods, building and engineering material, leather manufactures, paints, paper, stationary, chemicals, medicines, etc.

In total, the Ottawa Agreement was more beneficial to U.K. than to India. During the operation of the scheme, British imports in India increased by 34 per cent, while Indian exports to Britain increased by only 7.5 per sent. People also realized that imperial preference made India dependent on Empire markets than on foreign markets. In 1963, the Indian Legislative Assembly passed a resolution refusing to continue with the Ottawa Agreement and urged its termination. But, the viceroy of India, with his special powers, continued it till 1939 when a *New Indo-British trade Agreement* was signed which modified the Ottawa agreement in some particulars. According to this trade agreement, a number of articles like tobacco, food, drink, raw materials, and semi-manufactured goods were excluded from preferential treatment. India gave a preference of 10 per cent to a number of British imports, like chemicals, woolen carpets, sewing machines and 7.5 per cent on motor cars, motor cycles, cycles, buses, etc. in return Britain allowed the free import of lac, raw jute, mica, etc., and gave a preference of 10 per cent advalorem to linseed, castor-seed, groundnuts, leather, spices, etc., a preference 15 per cent to jute manufacturers, oils, and a preference of 20 per cent on cotton manufacturers, like sacks and bags. Specified rates of preference were given to a number of articles, like tea, coffee, rice, etc.

The Agreement was entirely denounced by the public as it prevented any trade agreement being concluded with any other country in as much of all concessions had been granted to Britain. Further, it was felt that it would adversely affect the Indian cotton mill industry and also the balance of payments position.

The Second World War was a blessing in disguise, and it put an end to the controversies of trade policy. India pained Independence which enabled her to formulate an independent commercial policy to promote the economic interests of India. After independence, India chose to be a full-fledged member of the British Commonwealth, and the system of Imperial Preference was adopted under the name '*Commonwealth preference*'. Before the Second World War, International trade agreements were mostly bilateral and all discriminatory treatment in respect of tariffs and the quantum of goods imported was settled by mutual negotiations. As a consequence, there was no restriction on dumping or subsidised exports. This resulted in good deal of competition. The more advanced and powerful nations were invariably at an advantage over backward nations. Hence, the need was felt for better international understanding and cooperation in economic sphere which resulted in the birth of *General Agreement on Trade and Tariffs (GATT).*

General Agreement on Trade and Tariffs (G.A.T.T.)

The Bretton Woods Conference of Nations held in 1944 gave birth to the concepts of *International Monetary Fund (IMF)* to help countries with balance of payments difficulties and problems;and also *International Bank for Reconstruction and Development* (IBRD, otherwise known as World Bank) to help the reconstruction of economies ravaged by the Second World War and the development of the developing economies by providing long-term financial assistance. These concepts were given shape and the IMF and the World Bank were established in 1946. At this juncture, the need for *International Trade Organisation (ITO)* was also felt.

Accordingly, a world conference was held in 1947 at Havana which led to the signing of the well known HAVANA CHARTER relating to the International Trade Organisation (I.T.O.). India was one of the original signatories of the charter. The aim of the charter was the removal of reduction of tariffs by the member countries. But the charter was never ratified and the proposal to establish the ITO was abandoned in 1951 on an account of opposition from the United States and United Kingdom.

Meanwhile in 1947, 23 nations met at Geneva and drew up a plan for the reduction of import duties and also against future increase in duties by the negotiating countries. This came to be known as the General Agreement of Trade and Tariffs. It came into effect on a provisional basis on July 9, 1948. The GATT was not a statute to be compulsorily enforced on member countries, but an instrument forged by common consent and adhered to voluntarily by them. It was an intergovernmental instrument, providing for rights and obligations in the field of commercial policy of the member countries with the principal object of promoting international trade through reciprocal and mutually advantageous arrangements by reducing trade barriers, customs, tariffs and discriminatory practices. In short, the GATT *stood for promotion of free, non-discriminatory, multilateral trade and for abolishing all unfair trade practices.*

If there were overwhelming reasons for a country to seek relief from any commitment, it was assured of fair consideration under special provisions. The salient feature of the GATT was the spirit of frankness and accommodation with which new arrangements were arrived at in annual conferences on the basis of representations and complaints of member countries.

Objectives of GATT

The objectives of GATT agreement were based on some fundamental principles contained in Code of International conduct. The salient principles and objectives of GATT can be enumerated as below:

(i) The international trade should be carried on the basis of non-discrimination, reciprocity and transparency.

(ii) The protection to the domestic industries should be given only by means of tariffs and by no other means.

(iii) The Most Favoured Nation (MFN) principles should be followed by all the members. The members should enter into consultations for the avoidance of damage to the interests of the members.

(iv) The multilateral negotiations should be carried to reduce tariff and non-tariff barriers to trade.

The framework of these principles has been amplified as follows.

(a) To encourage full employment and large and steadily growing volume of real income and effective demand;

(b) To ensure the full use of world resources.

(c) To bring about the expansion of world production and exchange.

(d) To bring about a steady improvement in the living standards of people in member countries; and

(e) To settle the disputes through consultation within the framework of GATT.

For achievement of these, the preamble of the GATT agreement required the members to enter "into reciprocal and mutually advantageous arrangements directed to the substantial reduction of tariff and other barriers to trade and to the elimination of discrimination treatment in international commerce".

Provisions of G.A.T.T.

In order to realize the above stated principles and objectives, GATT has made the following provisions:

Most Favoured Nation (MFN) Clause: The significant provision of GATT was the 'Most Favoured Nation' clause, which connotes that all contracting parties of the Agreement would be considered as most favoured nations and the benefits extended to one, should also be extended to all contracting parties. In short, there should be no discrimination among the nations, and trading should be carried on the principle of non-discrimination and reciprocity. In essence, this clause discouraged the member countries from granting any new trade concessions, unless those were multilaterally agreed.

However, there were several 'Escape Clauses'. The less developed countries were assured of the right to discriminate under certain specific circumstances. For instance, dumping and export subsidy might be countered by trade measures, only against the offending country. Further, special concessions were allowed for trade with former colonies of developed Western countries.

Quantitative Restrictions on Imports: The GATT rules, as a matter of principle, prohibited the use of import quota fixation and import licenses, under Article XI of the GATT agreements. However, there were exceptions.

To this rule, under specific circumstances: (a) Countries which were facing balance of payments difficulties could use the device of import quota fixation. But this quota should be limited only to the extent necessary to stop a serious decline in foreign exchange reserves. The IMF should be consulted in this matter. (b) Under-developed countries might resort to quota fixation, only under the procedure approved by the GATT. (c) Quotas might be applied to agricultural and fishery products, if domestic production was subject to equally restrictive controls. (d) When a foreign country was exporting products at artificially low (dumped) prices or at the subsidised prices, the affected country was allowed by the GATT to take suitable projective action. (e) The countries were allowed to form Customs Union or free trade under Article XXIV of the GATT agreement, provided their aim was to promote trade among the constituent countries, and not to raise trade barriers against other contracting parties.

Tariff Negotiations and Tariff Reduction: GATT considered that tariffs were the important obstacle to international trade and therefore, encouraged negotiations for the reduction of high tariffs. The negotiations for the reduction of tariff should be conducted on a reciprocal and mutually advantageous basis, taking into consideration the varying needs of individual contacting parties. Article II of the GATT specified that all concessions granted by contracting parties, as a consequence of negotiations, must be entered in a '*Schedule of Concessions;* A concession might assume the form of a reduction in the rate of import tariff or an agreement to bind, i.e., not to like the existing rate of duty. Once a concession was included in the schedule concessions, it could not be withdrawn except under specified circumstances. It meant that provisions of schedule of concessions, binding clause and tariff negotiations created a strong in-built bias towards the lowering down of rates of import tariff in the GATT. The negotiation procedure concerning tariff reduction was bilateral-multilateral. It was bilateral as two contracting parties entered into negotiation for tariff reduction on a selective commodity-to-commodity basis. The tariff reduction agreed between any two negotiations parties was to be made applicable to all the contracting parties under the 'Most Favoured Nation' clause. This was the multilateral aspect of tariff negotiations.

Subsides and Countervailing Duties: It was recognized by the GATT that the subsidies were alternative to tariff. The Tokyo Round of the GATT in 1970s considered it necessary to specify the code of conduct related to subsidies. The industrial countries agreed to a complete ban on export subsidies in the case of manufactured products. The LDC (Least Developed Countries) were however, exempted from this stipulation. The member countries were required to avoid subsidies on the export of primary products in principle. In case they provided subsidies on the export of primary products, that should be done in such a manner that the country employing them did not acquire a more than equitable share in the world export of the concerned products. In case the subsidies resulted in harm to the interest of importing countries, the agreement authorised them to take resort to countervailing duties. In case any country was found to take recourse to dumping, i.e., the export price of a product was lower than its domestic price; the affected country was allowed to impose the countervailing or anti-dumping duties to the extent that the dumping got neutralized. However, the country resorting to countervailing or anti-dumping duties should not impose duties at a higher rate than was required to offset the margin of dumping and the affected industry in the importing country should not acquire thereby a net additional protection.

Complaints and Waivers: Article XXII of the GATT made provision for dealing with any complaint from a contraction party related to the operation of the Agreement. The complainant could request the other party for consultation, if the former felt that the action of the latter has provided injurious and the former could not reap the benefits under the GATT Agreement. Article XXV of the GATT laid down the procedure for granting waiver to some contracting party, form the application of the provisions of the GATT. Ordinarily, the waivers were not granted unless those approved by two-thirds of the voting contracting parties.

Settlement of Disputes: The GATT had provisions for the settlement of disputes among the contracting parties. Initially, the contracting parties would hold talks on bilateral basis to resolve the disputed matter. In case of failure, the matter could be referred to a panel of experts drawn from countries having no direct interest in the matter. This panel or committee, after a careful study, used to make a recommendation or ruling to be observed by the offending party. In case the offending party did not comply with the ruling or did not act upon the recommendations of the panel, the aggrieved party was authorized to retaliate by withdrawing some or all concessions offered to the offending country. Thus, dispute settlement procedures of the GATT rested upon direct consultations, conciliation and third party adjudication. GATT had generally proved successful, in resolving disputes among the contracting parties.

Since 1947, global conferences were held by the GATT for the purpose of global trade negotiations and these conferences are called Rounds. The first conference on trade negotiations was held at Geneva in 1947, the second at Annecy (France) in 1949, Third at Torquay (England) in 1950-51, the forth at Geneva in 1955-56, the fifth at Geneva between 1961-62, (Dillon

Round), the sixth at Geneva, known as Kennedy Round, (1963-67), the seventh at Tokyo (Japan) (1973-79) and the Eighth at Punta del Estes in Uruguay, Known as Uruguay Round, which converted GATT into W.T.Q., with effect from 1995.

In the first five Rounds, over 60,000 tariff rates were reviewed and settled. Between 1948 and 1962 the world trade became double in real terms. The average growth rate in international trade in terms of volumes was 10 per cent per annum and in terms of value was 13 per cent per annum, white the world output was increasing at 5.5 per cent per annum.

Since most of these Rounds could not be considered very important, we shall confine only with three of these Rounds, *viz.*, the Kennedy Round, the Tokyo Round and the Uruguay Round which had contributed substantially towards the progress and development of GATT.

The Sixth Round of GATT: Kennedy Round

The sixth conference of GATT (1963-67) popularly known as Kennedy Round was held at Geneva in which 54 countries participated for trade negotiations. This conference was held at the initiative of president Kennedy of USA, and hence the name Kennedy Round. President Kennedy took the initiative in securing concessions from EEC. EEC and the USA were complaining against each other's protective measures. The results of Kennedy Round include the tariff reduction by the advanced countries like the USA, the EEC countries, Japan and Canada on an average to the extent of 35 per cent. The incidence of tariff reduction was not uniform in case of different groups of commodities. The maximum tariff cut had been extended in case of chemicals, paper, etc. in the case of products like iron and steel, fuels, textiles, the tariff cut was very minimum. In addition, the deliberations were held on non-tariff barriers, agriculture and tariff reeducation on the exportable products of the LDCs. No doubt, the Kennedy Round of the GATT could make a significant contribution in effecting substantial tariff cuts; yet the achievements were still short of the objective.

The Seventh Round of GATT: Tokyo Round

The seventh GATT conference was held at Tokyo (1973-79) and hence the name Tokyo Round. This conference deliberated upon the issues including tariff reductions, removal of non-tariff barriers, coordinated scaling down of all trade barriers in selected sectors, trade liberalisation in agriculture, etc.

Tariff Reduction: The tariff reduction agreed by the leading countries such as the USA, the EEC and Japan, on an average, was of the magnitude of 31 per cent, 27 per cent and 28 per cent respectively. The negotiated tariff reduction by the contracting parties was to be phased over 8 years commencing from 1980.

Non-tariff Barriers: The Tokyo Round laid down a code of conduct for nations to follow in respect of non-tariff barriers. This code included (a) agreement on a code about the government procurements, (b) uniformity in the application of duties in countervailing and antidumping cases, and (c) a generalized system of preferences to the manufactured, semi-manufactured and selected other exports of the LCD's countries. However, many products such as textiles, shoes, consumer electronics, steel and several other products that were of very vital interest for the LCD's remained excluded.

Removal of Technical Barriers: An agreement was reached through Tokyo Round about the removal of unnecessary trade barriers existing in the form of technical standards. The provision in the agreement was made concerning complaints related to the violation of the code of technical standard by the contraction parties and redressed thereof.

Import Licensing Procedures: The Tokyo Round resulted in an agreement concerning the simplification of import licensing procedures. It provided for automatic grant of approval of the application on the inflow of goods, simplification of licensing procedure in case of quota and other import restrictions. It also provided for creating institutions and procedures for consultation and settlement of disputes between the contracting parties.

Customs Valuation: An agreement was reached among the nations providing for a fair, natural and uniform system for the valuation of goods for customs purposes.

Trade Related Investment Measures (TRIMs). The most outstanding feature was the inclusion of the last subject referred to above. The UR went much beyond mere trading goods by including services, Technology, Investment and Information.

World Trade Organisation (W.T.O)

According to the Agreement made by the Uruguay Round, GATT was converted into an international Organisation called World Trade Organisation (WTO) with effect from January 1, 1995. This WTO will serve as a single institutional framework encompassing GATT and also all the results of the Uruguay Round. WTO will be directed by a Ministerial Conference that will meet at least once every two years. Its regular business will be overseen by a General Council.

Objective of W.T.O.

Inheriting the principles of GATT, the world trade Organizations, based in Geneva, Switzerland, professes the following basic objectives:

1. Raising the standard of living and incomes, promoting full employment, expanding production and trade, and optimum utilization of world's resources.
2. Introducing sustainable development- a concept which envisages that development and environment can go together.
3. Taking positive steps to ensure that developing countries, especially the least developed ones, secure a better share of growth in world trade.

Functions of W.T.O.

1. It shall provide the necessary framework for the implementation, administration and operation of Trade agreements made on multilateral basis. It should also

facilitate the actual implementation, administration of the Multilateral Trade Agreements and thereby promote the objectives of these trade agreements.

2. The WTO shall make necessary arrangements to provide negotiation facilities among the member countries concerning their multilateral trade relations and matters of agreements.
3. WTO shall administer the *'Understanding on Rules and Procedures Governing the Settlement of Disputes'*.
4. It is its duty to administer the 'Trade Review Mechanism'.
5. It is the duty of WTO to cooperate appropriately with the IMF and IBRD and its affiliated agencies to achieve greater coherence with them in shaping the global economic policy.

The General Council of the WTO is entrusted with the following functions; viz.,

(a) Supervising on a regular basis the operation of the revised agreements and ministerial declarations relating to (i) goods; (ii) services; and (iii) TRIPs.

(b) Acting as a Dispute Settlement Body.

(c) Serving as a Trade Review Mechanism; and

(d) Establishing Goods Council, Service Council and TRIPs Council as subsidiary bodies.

From the above mentioned functions of the WTO, it is evident that this is a more powerful body with enlarged functions than the GATT. The WTO is expected to play a major role in the world economic affairs.

It should be noted here that a country can become a member of the WTO by fully accepting all the results of the Uruguay Round.

The old GATT system was flexible, adjustable, giving ample scope for the member countries to have ample elbow rooms in their international trade and also in agreements. Under the old GATT system, the member countries were allowed to continue with their domestic legislations, even if they violated a GATT agreement. This was done under the grandfather clause of the old GATT which accepted the member country as a signatory to GATT by allowing exceptions. On the other hand, the WTO totally prohibited this and ruled out any domestic legislations which are violate of agreements arrived at under Uruguay Round.

India was not only a founder member of GATT; it is a signatory in the WTO. India faces several issues which have to be settled down in WTO meetings in the interest of national economy.

Trade Related Aspects of Intellectual Property Rights: (TRIPs)

There are several controversial outcomes in the Uruguay Round Agreements. Of these, the most controversial is the agreement on Trade related aspects of intellectual property rights, otherwise known as known as TRIPs. As a matter of fact, TRIPs along with TRIMs have become issues in the UR, and several contradictory and also confusing opinions are expressed about these clauses.

Intellectual Property Rights may be defined as "Information with a commercial value". This is characterized be "ideas, inventions and creative expression" including the "public willingness to bestow the status of property on them and give owners the right to exclude others from access to or use of protected subject matter." In other words, Intellectual Property Rights (IPRs) may be legally protected by patents, copyrights, industrial designs, geographical indications and trade marks. Special forms of protection have also emerged to address specific needs of knowledge producers as in the case of plant breeder's rights and the protection of layout designs of integrated circuits. A number of countries also have trade secret laws to protect undisclosed that gives a competitive advantages to its owner.

Several critics are of the view that TRIPs as embodied in the agreement will have very serious and also disastrous effects on Indian economy, particularly in the areas of agriculture and pharmaceuticals. Under TRIPs, patents shall be available for any invention, whether product or process in all fields of industrial technologies. Patent protection will be extended to micro-organisms, non-biological and micro-biological processes and plant varieties. This implies that the entire industrial agricultural sectors and to some extent bio-technology sector will be covered under the patent provisions. A very dangerous provision has been introduced in patent protection and this relates to changing the philosophy of the patent regime whereby products, imported or locally produced, will be covered under patent protection without any discrimination. This implies that the patent regime will not only try to establish manufacturing monopoly, but also establish import monopoly. In this situation, the patent holder would resort to imports only and the national government would not be able to exercise any price control on the imported products. This provision will help the patent holder to defy all price control measures.

According to critics, this patent regime will affect the drug price seriously in India. They contend that at present the prices of drugs are very low in India when compared to other foreign countries, due to the operation of Indian Patent Act, 1970.

Indian pharmaceutical and drug industry developed and progressed very rapidly and successfully under the above stated Patent Act 1970 so as to provide several life-saving drugs at a very cheap rate, when compared to other countries, besides earning good foreign exchange exceeding Rs. 2000 crores per year.

According to B.K. Keayla, Convener, National Working Group on Patent Laws, more than 70 per cent of the drugs will be covered under the new patent laws. Consequently, under TRIPs, heavy payments will have to be made to patent holders and this would result in the prices of drugs going up several times. We know that majority of the people in India are very poor and they cannot afford to buy modern drugs for their health cover and safety. Even with the prevailing low prices of drugs, only 35 per cent of the population could afford modern drugs and if the GATT agreement is accepted, still larger proportion of the population may have to lose health cover, as only the highest income-group alone could afford increased prices of drugs. The drugs are under process patent in India, while it is under product patent in countries like U.K.,

U.S.A., and Pakistan. As a consequence of product patent regime, the price differential of important drugs ranges 10 to 15 times more in these countries than what is India. For example, the drug Ranitidine (Zantac Brand) marketed by Glaxo costs about Rs. 30/- (300mg x 10's) in India, whereas the same drug costs Rs. 260/- in Pakistan, Rs. 480/- in U.K., and Rs. 744/- in U.S.A (Prices are converted into Indian Rupees). Similarly, the drug Diclofenac (Voveran Brand) marketed by Ciba costs Rs. 6/- (50mg x 10's) in India, whereas the drug costs Rs. 55/- in Pakistan, Rs. 95/- in U.K. and Rs. 239/- in U.S.A. We can very well calculate the price differential between the prices prevailing in India and the other countries mentioned. If these drugs are product patend as in foreign countries, the MNCs would be selling at a fantastic price, as done in other countries. The Government of India had indicated that as a result of the Dunkel Final Act, drug prices in India would increase by 10 to 15 per cent only. Country like India which does not recognize product patent in the field of drugs, food products and chemicals, a transitional period of 10 years has been given for establishing a product patent regime. Further, the Government of India avers that the prices would not be allowed to increase very much and it will be controlled through price control measures on drugs. In practice, however, this may not be strictly possible. The MNCs can very easily contrive situations of artificial scarcity of these drugs. As a matter of fact, the drug market in India is now facing the phenomenon of disappearance later at a higher price. During the course of the period 1995 to 2000, the price indeed of drugs and medicines has increased around 78 percent, whereas the overall price index gone up only by 29 per cent. This rise in prices has taken place in spite of drug price control.

Hence, the argument of the Government that the new patent regime would result only in the price increase around 10 to 15 per cent only is altogether untenable.

However, not all share this view of pessimism and contend that there is too much of exaggeration about the supposed increase in prices of drugs and medicines due to patent regime. According to the counter critics, the cross-country comparisons of prices of drugs should not be taken too seriously. The Essential Drugs List published by the WHO has only around 250 entries. Less than 10 per cent of these are covered by patents world-wide. The rest have all become generic and there is nod need to grant a fresh round of patent protection to these. According to Bibek Debory, the price rise will be pertinent only in the case of these existing drugs, but not for the new drugs that arrive on the international market every year. If the patent protection is not changed, these new drugs may not be marketed in India at all. Economists and critics do not agree with these points on the outcome of the policy of patent regime. The Government has to continue with the Drug Price Control Order so far as essential drugs are concerned. Otherwise, several essential medicines will become beyond the reach of poor and middle classes.

Finally, according to Indian Law, there is ceiling on the royalty or fee that a patent holder can demand from a license. But in TRIPs there can be no ceiling on the fee or royalty that can be demanded from a license by the patent holder.

In this context, the major area of concern is the possibility of large-scale biopiracy of India's herbal wealth by foreign firms. We known, India is a land of abundant herbal wealth and several plants having medicinal and curative properties. Ours is the land of Ayurveda, the system of ancient medicines and curing with the help of herbal wealth of the country. Basic ingredients of several medicines are turmeric, Tulsi, Bilva, Neem, Ginger, Pepper, Phyllanthus Amarus (Keelanelli in Tamil), Senna, Aml etc., besides hundreds of varieties of roots and herbs. These are available in India. Many of these medicinal plants, herbs, roots and barks of trees are not patented and India does not have a Sui generic system for its protection. The absence of a legal mechanism to protect our heritage of common knowledge and even what are there in the ancient books and scripts may lead to biopiracy by firms or individuals in developed countries as happened in the case of granting patent for the "invention" in the USA that numeric promotes healing and neem has insecticidal and pesticide properties.

We know that turmeric is the native plant of India and this is used since ancient days in out day-to-day life. It is an important requisite in out cultural, spiritual and religious activities, besides being an important material in the kitchen and also in Ayurvedic medicines. This ubiquitous 'turmeric' was sought to be patented under the American Law in 1995. Fortunately for India, the Director General of Council of Scientific and Industrial Research, Dr. R.A., Mashelkar challenged this attempt. Finally, the U.S. patent office acknowledged its mistake and cancelled the patent on 'turmeric'. An American Company has been given patent right for Neem as a pesticide. We know Basmati rice is a very popular and also universal variety in our country. This Basmati has been patented as Kasmati and Texmati. These examples are only indications of possible bio-piracy of India's ancient plants and herbs. India has to take every precaution by means of hug documentation about the use of plant and herbal wealth of the country.

Trade Related Investment Measures (TRIMs)

Another important area where the sovereignty of developing countries has been restricted and also curbed in the U.R. According is what is called Trade Related Investment Measures, in short, TRIMs. What do you mean by TRIMs? This refers to certain conditions or restrictions imposed by a government in respect of foreign investment in their countries would make certain conditions and restrictions like percentage of foreign equity, utilization of local materials in the manufactures and also some conditions regarding export of finished goods to foreign countries to earn foreign exchange. Almost every developing country was widely using this TRIMs, including India, to regulate foreign investment so as to benefit economic growth of the country.

The U.R. Agreement on TRIMs provides that no contracting country shall apply any TRIM which is inconsistent with the W.T.O. Articles. An illustrative list of the U.R. Agreement identifies the following TRIMs as inconsistent:

(1) Local content requirement: The country should not impose any restrictions of local inputs to be used in

products. Generally, developing countries would insist on using their indigenous materials by the Multinational Corporations in their productive processes. But, according to U.R. Agreement, this is prohibited. The foreign investments should not be tied with such conditions in trade.

(2) Trade Balancing requirement: According to this, the member countries of U.R. Agreement should not impose any restriction on the quantum of imports, i.e., conditions like imports shall not exceed a certain proportion of exports.

(3) Trade and Foreign exchange balancing requirements: The member countries of the Agreement should not make any attempt or pass laws restricting trade activities to balance foreign exchange requirements.

(4) Domestic sales Requirements: The member countries of the WTO prohibited from making any restrictions that the foreign companies should sell a certain proportion of their output locally.

The U.R. Agreement categorically states that member countries of the WTO should abolish any laws inconsistent with the agreement and any restrictions related to TRIMs should be withdrawn in a phased manner. The WTO gave two years time for industrialized countries, five years time for developing countries and seven years time for least developed countries as transition period to phase out all restrictions of their TRIMs inconsistent with WTO. Transition period can be extended for developing and least developed countries, if they face difficulties in eliminating TRIMs.

Implications of these on India

The main provisions enunciated in the TRIMs of the U.R. Agreement of WTO have enormous implications and also impact on the country of any developing country like India.

(a) The TRIMs text of WTO wants to ensure that all member Governments shall not discriminate against foreign capital. In other words, member countries should give national treatment to foreign capital without any bar or restrictions. All restrictions on foreign capital or investing companies should be scrapped out.

(b) All foreign investors in the country shall be given same rights in the matter of investment as a national investor and no restrictions will be imposed on any area of investment.

Export Finance

Introduction

Though banks are providing different types of loans to customers, export finance is a kind of advance by which not only the customer is benefited but also the country itself as it brings valuable foreign exchange earnings. Hence, government has give more importance to export finance and has simplified various procedures involved in obtaining finance. Reserve Bank of India has also given instructions to commercial banks that they should give top priority in the sanctioning of export finance.

Institutions involved in Export Finance

Numbers of institutions have not only emerged in providing export finance but even the existing institutions have opened up various avenues in granting export finance. The institutions are:

(1) Export import bank

(2) Commercial banks, both nationalized and non-nationalized

(3) Development banks such as IDBI, ICICI, etc.

(4) Small Industries Development Bank of India.

(5) State Finance Corporations.

(6) National Small Industries Corporation.

(7) Export Credit Guarantee Corporation.

All the above institutions are providing finance for exporters directly a well as directly. They are also guaranteeing for the loans given by foreign banks. The foreign banks are giving offshore lending which our Indian banks are yet to take up. In offshore lending, loans are given in foreign exchange enabling the foreign buyers to purchase goods from the domestic producer. There is also export finance given to deemed exports which consists of finance made available to those who are supplying raw materials or semi finished goods to foreign companies operating in India. Especially in export processing zones or in free trade zones.

Different Types of Export Finance

The following are the different types of finance made available by the various institutions mentioned above.

1. Pre-shipment export finance
2. Post-shipment export finance
3. Export finance against collection of bills
4. Export finance against deferred payment
5. Export finance against allowances and subsidies.

Pre-shipment Export Finance

Under the Foreign Exchange Regulation Act (FERA) which is now amended as Foreign Exchange Management (FEMA). Every exporter must obtain from the foreign importer, irrevocable letter of credit which is issued by the importer's bank. Against this letter of credit (LC), loan is given by the domestic bank to the exporter. Sometimes in anticipation of the letter of credit, an anticipatory letter of credit is received and loans are given to the exporter. There is also a package credit given to the exporter to meet his entire credit right from the purchase of raw material till the shipment of the finished product. Even to obtain the shipping order, loan is granted which is for reserving berth for shipping the goods.

Post-shipment Export Finance

After the shipment of goods, the bills are handed over to the bank by the exporter. The bank has three options.

(i) The bills may be purchased by which the bank will pay full value of the export bill to the exporter. The risk is now transferred to the bank form the exporter.

Or

(ii) The bank will discount the bill which depends upon the country to which the bill belongs to.

Or

(i) The bank will neither purchase nor discount but will send the bill for collection and will credit the account of the customer only on realization.

The treatment of the bills depends on the country to which it belongs to. The bills drawn on importers of developed countries will be purchased.

Example: U.K., U.S.A.

Bills drawn on countries which are politically stable but economically weak will be discounted. Example: Egypt, Sri Lanka, India.

Countries which are weak both politically and economically. Example: West African Countries, Rwanda, Sierra lone, Congo. Bills will be only collected and then credited.

Export Finance Against Collection of Bills

When the bills are in the process of collection and where the bank knows the fate of the bill, the bank will extend finance to the exporter.

Export Finance Against Deferred Payment

The finance here is on the basis of installment payment. There are two types of finance, namely, suppliers' credit and buyers' credit.

In the case of suppliers credit banks in India will finance the exporters to sell on installment basis or hire purchase basis to the importers. The exporter will be willing to de so due to the finance given to him by banks. Example: Railway coaches are exported from India to African countries under this type of credit.

In the case of buyers credit the financial institution in India will provide a line of credit which is the form of loan to the borrowing country, which in turn gives to the Central bank of the country, which lends to commercial banks and ultimately to the importer. Thus, the buyer is given credit for purchasing capital goods on installment basis. As it is a line of credit, the repayment responsibility rests with the borrowing country.

Export Finance Against Allowances and Subsidies

By way of encouraging the exporters, government has come forward to provide subsidies and allowances. A subsidy is a reduction in the cost of the exporter. For example, if a cycle factory sells cycles at a low price in foreign country in view of the competition, the government has to subsidies the price of raw material, *i.e.*, steel to the exporter of cycles. This is known as import parity reimbursement price. There is a difference between the international price of steel and domestic market. This difference is given as subsidy.

Allowances

When the exporters is faced with a sudden increase in expenditure due it reasons beyond his control, the government comes forward to provide cash compensatory support which is a percentage of costs of his finished product.

Example; deviation in the shipping route due to war.

Certain exports are made after importing raw material and they converted into finished product upon which its value increases manifold. For example, gold is imported and concerted into jewels after embedding precious stones. The cost of the jewel goes up. The exporter in this case is given a percentage of the export value as replenishment license by which he can import any item from foreign country, free of duty.

There is also export finance given to deemed exports i.e., in free trade zones at Mumbai, Chennai, Delhi, Cochin and Vizag, the supplies of goods to foreign exporters are given finance. In these free trade zones, the value of the goods exported should be not less than 50% from the domestic market. Hence, the suppliers are provided finance under deemed export finance.

In the year 2000, the government has come forward to start economic zones in Gujarat and Tamilnadu for the purpose of increasing exports. Banks will come forward to increase exports. There is also a pass book facility available to the exporter for continuous finance from the banks.

Review Questions

1. Explain the role of GATT and WTO in promoting Global Marketing.
2. Write the objectives and functions of WTO.
3. Explain TRIPS and TRIMS.

REFERENCES

Adler, Lee (1975), "Managing Marketing Research in the Diversified Multinational Corporation, "In Edward M. Mazze, Ed. Marketing in Turbulent Times and Marketing: The Challenges and Opportunities—Combined Proceedings. Chicago: American Marketing Association, 305-308.

Alexandar, Nicholas (1997), International Retailing, Oxford, UK: Blackwell Business.

Allen, Randy L. (1993), "The Why and How of Global Retailing." *Business Quarterly*, 57, No. 4 (Summer), 117-122.

Alster, Judith, and Holly Gallo (1992), "Corporate Strategies for Global Competitive Advantage", Reader's Digest Association Conference Board, Working Papers No.996.

Barnet, Richard J. and John Cavanagh (1994), Global Dreams Imperial Corporations and the New World Order Newyork: Simon and Schuster.

Bassiry, G.R. and R. Hrair Dekmejian (1993), "America's Global Companies: A Leadership Profile", *Business Horizons*, 36, No. 1 (January-February), 47-53.

Burgess, Steven M. (1998), The New Marketing Halfway House. South Africa: Zebra Press.

Botan, Carl (1992), "International Public Relations: Critique and Reformulation", *Public Relations Review*, 18, No. 2 (Summer), 149-159.

Bovet, Susan Fry (1994), "Building and International Team", *Public Relations Journal* (August/September), 26-28.

Bauer, P. T. (1954), West African Trade. Cambridge: Cambridge University Press.

Bello, Daniel C., and Ritu Lohita (1995), "Export Channel Design: The Use of Foreign Distributors and Agents." *Journal of the Academy of Marketing Science*, 23, No. 2, 83-93.

Burns, David J., and John T. Brady (1996), "Retail Ethics as Appraised by Future Business Personnel in Malaysia and the United States," *Journal of Consumer Affairs*, 30, No. 1, p. 195+.

Cavusgil, S. Tamer (1987), "Qualitative Insights into Company Experiences in International Marketing Research *Journal of Business and Industrial Marketing* (Summer), 41-54.

Crossen, Cynthia (1994), Tainted Truth: The Manipulation of Fact in America.Upper Saddie River, NJ: Simon & Schuster.

Czinkota, M. R. and I. A. Ronkainen (1994), "Market Research for Your Export Operations, Part I." International Trade Forum, 3: 22-33.

Czinkota, M. R., and I. A. Ronkainen. "Market Research for Your Export Operations, Part II. "International Trade F.

Chen, Zhengyi (1999), "Marketing Globally: Planning and Practice," *Journal of International Marketing*, 7, No. 2, 96-98.

Carr, Mark, Arlene Hostrop, and Daniel O'Cornor (1998), "The New Era of Global Retailing," *Journal of Business Strategy*, 19, and 3 :11-15.

Cavusgil, S. Tamer (1990), "The Importance of Distributor Training at Caterpillar. "Industrial Marketing Management, 19, No. 1 (February), 1-9.

Cornwell, T. Bettina, and Isabelle Maignan (1998), " An International Review of Sponsorship Research," *Journal of Advertising*, 27, No. 1 :1.

Davenport, Thomas H., Michael Hammer, and Tauno J. Metsisto (989), "How Executives Can Shape Their Company's Information Systems." *Harvard Business Review*, 67 (March/April), 1:130-134.

Davidson, Lawrence S. (1989), "Knowing the Unknowable" *Business Horizons*, 32 (September/October), 2-8.

Douglas, Susan P., C. Samuel Craig, and Warren J. Keegan (1982), "Approaches to Assessing International Marketing Opportunities for Small-and Medium Sized Companies," *Columbia Journal of World Business*, 2-30.

Dowling, Grahame R., Mark Uncles (1997), "Do Customer Loyalty Programs Really Work?" *Sloan Management Review*, 38, No. 4 :71.

Easton, Simon, and Penny Mackie (1998), "When Football Came Home: A Case History of the Sponsorship Activity at Euro '96." *International Journal of Advertising,* 17, No. 1, 99-114.

Epley, Joe S. (1992), "Public Relations in the Global Village: An American Perspective." *Public Relations Review,* 18, No. 2 (Summer), 109-116.

Fields, George(1983), From Bonsal to Levi's: An Insider's Surprising Account of How the Japanese Live New York: Macmillan.

Grunig, Larissa A. (1992), "Strategic Public Relations constituencies on a Global Scale," *Public Relations Review,* 18, No. 2 (Summer), 127-136.

Gilad, Benjamin (1989), "The Role of Organized Competitive Intelligence in Corporate Strategy," *Columbia Journal of World Business,* (Winter), 29-35.

Glazer, Rashi (19991), "Marketing in an Information-Intensive Environment: Strategic Implications of Knowledge as an Asset." Journal of Marketing (October), 1-19.

Green, Robert, and Eric Langeard (1975), "A Cross-National Comparison of Consumer Habits and Innovator Characteristics." *Journal of Marketing,* (July), 34-41.

Garland, Barbara C. and Marti J. Rhea (1988), "American Consumers: Profile of an Import Preference Segment," *Akron Business and Economic Review,* 19, No. 2 , 20-29.

Green, Paul E., and Abba M. Krieger (1991), "Segmenting Markets with Conjoint Analysis," *Journal of Marketing,* 55, No. 4 (October), 20-31.

Hout, Thomas, Michael E. Porter, and Eeleen Rudden (1982), "How Global Companies Win Out," *Harvard Business Review,* (September/October), 98-108.

Halal, William E. (1993), "Global Strategic Management in a New World Order, "*Business Horizons,* 36 (November-December), 5-10.

Herschell, Gordon Lewis, and Carol, Nelson (1998), Advertising Age Handbook of Advertising. Chicago: NTC Business Books, .

Hiebert, Ray E. (1994), "Advertising and Public Relations in Transition from Communism: The Case of Hungary, 1989-1994," *Public Relations Review,* 20, No. 4 (Winter), 357-372.

Honeycutt, Earl D. John B. Ford, and Lew Kurtzman (1996), "Potential Problems and Solutions When Hiring and Training a Worldwide Sales Team, "*Journal of Business & Industrial Marketing,* (Winter), 42.

Hanson, Ward (2000), Principles of Internet Marketing. Cincinnatti: South Western College Publishing.

Hill, John S. Richard R. Still, and Unal O. Boya (1991), "Managing the Multinational Sales Force," *International Marketing Review*, 8, No. 1, 19-31.

Hassan, Salah S. and Roger D. Blackwell (1994), Global Marketing Orlando, FL: The Dryden Press, .

Johansson, Johny K., and Ikujiro Nonaka (1997), Relentless The Japanese Way of Marketing. New York: Harper Business.

Josephs, Ray, and Juanita W. Josephs (1994), "Public Relations, the U.K. Way," *Publlic Relations Journal,* (April), 14-18.

Kaikati, Jack G. (1993), "Don't Crack the Japanese Distribution System Just Circumvent It," *Columbia Journal of World Business,* 28, No. 2 (Summer), 34-45.

Kale, Sudhir and Roger P. McIntyre (1991), "Distribution Channel Relationships in Diverse Cultures," *International Marketing Review,* 8, No. 3, 311-345.

Klein, Saul, and Victor Roth (1993), "Satisfaction with International Marketing Channels," *Journal of the Academy of Marketing Science,* 21, No. 1, (Winter), 39-44.

Murphy, Paul R., James M. Daley, and Douglas R. Dalenberg (1993), "Doing Business in Global Markets: Perspectives of International Freight Forwarders," *Journal of Global Marketing,* 6, No. 4, 53-68.

Kaynak, Erdener (1998), "Sales Promotion Practices of Consumer Goods Companies in an Advanced Developing Country," *International Journal of Advertising,* 17, No. 2, 213-233.

Krckeberg, Dean (1996), "A Global Perspective on Public Relations Ethics: The Middle East," *Public Relations Review,* 22, No. 2 (Summer), 181-189.

Kucukemiroglu, Orsay, Erdener Kaynak, and Sevgu Ayse Ozturk (1998), "Sales and Promotion Practices of Consumer Goods Companies in an Advanced Developing Country," *International Journal of Advertising,* 17, No. 2, 213+.

Keegan, Warren J. and Bodo B. Schelegelmilch (2000), Global Marketing Management: A European Perspective. New York: Prentice Hall International.

Khanna, T. and K. Palepu (1997), "Why Focussed Strategies May be Wrong for Emerging Markets," *Harvard Business Review*, (July-August), 41-51.

Keegan, Warren J. (1967), "Scanning the International Business Environment: A Study of the Informational Acquisition Process," Doctorial Dissertation, Harvard Business School.

Kelly, John M. (1987), How to Check Out Your Competition: A Complete Plan for Investigating Your Market. New York: Wiley.

King, W. R. and V. Sethi (1993), "Developing Transnational Information Systems: A Case Study," Omega (January), 53-59.

Kravis, Irving B., Zoltan Kenessey, Alan Heston, and Robert Summers (1975), A System of International Comparisons of Gross Product and Purchasing Power, Balti-more: Johns Hopkins University Press.

Lewin, Jeffrey E., and Wesley J. Johnston (1997), "International Salesforce Management: A Relationship Perspective, *Journal of Business and Industrial Marketing*, 12, No. 3-4, (Summer), 232+.

Lindberg, Bertil C. "International Comparison of Growth in Demand for a New Durable Consumer Product."

Malnigh, T.W. (1995), "Globalization of an Ethnocentric Firm: An Evolutionary Perspective", *Strategic Management Journal*, 16 (February), 119-141.

Miles, Gregory L. (1995), "Tailoring a Global Product," *International Business*, (March), 5052.

Miller, L. K. (1992), Transnational Corporations: A Selective Bibiliography, 1991-1992. New York: United Nations.

Moyer, Reed (1982), "International Market Analysis," *Journal of Marketing Research*, (August), 364-371.

Mullen, Michael R (1995), "Diagnosing Measurement Equivalence in Cross-National Research," *Journal of International Business Studies*, 26 (Third Quarter), 573-596.

Miles, Gregory L. (1993), "Think Global, Go Internmodal," *International Business*, (March), 61.

Morwitz, Vicki G., and David Schmittlein (1992), "Using Segmentation to Improve Sales Forecasts Based on Purchase Intent: Which 'Intenders' Actually Buy?" *Journal of marketing Research*, 29, No. 4 (November), 391-405.

Nessmann, Karl (1995), "Public Relations in Europe: A Comparison with the United Statesm", *Public Relations Journal*, 21, No. 2, (Summer), 151-160.

Newsom, Doug and Bob Carrell (1994), "Professional Public Relations in India: Need Outstrips Supply," *Public Relations Journal*, 20, No. 2, (Summer), 183-188

Oisen, Janeen E., and Kent L. Granzin (1990), "Economic Development and Channel Structure: A Multinational Study," *Journal of Macromarketing*, 10, No. 2 , 61-77.

Ohmae, Kenichi (1995), The End of the Nation State: The Rise of Regional Economies, New York: The Free Press.

Pawle, John (1999), "Mining the International Consumer," *Journal of the Market Research Society*, 41, No. 1, 19-32.

Panigrahi, Bragaban, Ranjita Misra, and Stephen E. Calrish (1996), "Perceptions of Indian Business Organizations toward Formal Marketing Research," The International Executive, 38 (September/October), 613-632.

Piirto, Rebecca (1991), Beyond Mind Games. The Marketing Power of Psychographics. Ithaca, NY: American Demographics Books.

Raguraman K. and Claire Chan (1994), "The Development of Sea-Air Intermodal Transportation: An Assessment of Global Trends," *The Logistics and Transportations Review*, 30, No. 4, (December), 379-396.

"Retail Marketing: International Perspectives," *The European Journal of Marketing*, 26, No. 8/9 (1992), Special Issue.

Reich, Robert B. (1992), The Work of Nations, New York: Vintage Books.

Reid, David MeHardy (1995), "Perspectives for International Marketers on the Japanese Market," *Journal of International Marketing*, 3, No. 1, (1995), 63-64. orum, 31, No. 1, 16:21.

Raju, P. S., (1995), "Consumer Behavior in Global Markets: The A-B-C-D Paradigm and Its Application to Eastern Europe and the Third World," *Journal of Consumer Marketing*,12, No. 5, 37-56.

Sachdev, Harash J., Daniel C. Bello, and Bruce K. (1994), Pilling Distributionm," *Journal of Global Marketing,* 8, No. 2, 31-50.

Samiee, Saeed (1993), "Retailing and Channel Considerations in Devolopiкng Countries: A Review and Research Proposition," *Journal of Business Research,* 27, No. 2 (June), 103-129.

Sherwood, Charles, and Robert Bruns (1992), "Solving International Transportation Problems," *Review of Business,* 14, No. 1, (Summer/Fall), :25-30.

Stern, Louis W., and Adel L. EI- Ansary (1992), Marketing Channels, 4th ed. Upper Saddle River, NJ: Prentice Hall.

Sharpe, Melvin L (1992), "The Impact of Social and Cultural Conditioning on Global Public Relations," *Public Relations Review,* 18, No. 2, 103-107.

Shoham, Aviv (1999), "Performance in Trade shows and Exhibitions: A Synthesis and Directions for Future Research," *Journal of Global Marketing,* 12, No. 3, 41-57.

Stewart-Allen, Allyson L. (1999), "Cross-Border Conflicts of European Sales Promotions," *Marketing New,* 26 April, p. 10.

Sethi, S. Prakash (1971), "Comparitive Cluster Analysis for World Markets," *Joournal of Marketing Research,* 8 (August), 350.

Sharer, Kevin (1991), "Top Management's Intelligence Needs: Competitive Intelligence Review (Spring), 3-5.

Stanat, Ruth (1991), "Tracking Your Global Competition," *Competitive Intelligence Review,* (Spring), 17-19.

Steenkamp, Jan-Benedict E. M. (1998), "Assessing Measurement Invariance in Cross-National Consumer Research," *Journal of Consumer Research,* 25, No. 1, 78-91.

Simon, Herman (1996), Hidden Champions: Lessons from 500 of the World's Best Unknown Companies. Boston, M.A: Harvard Business School Press.

Sonnenberg, Frank K. (1990), Marketing to Win: Strategies for Building Competitive Advantage in Service Industries New York: Harper Business.

Ter Hofstede, Frenkel, Jan-benedict E. M. Steenkamp, and Michael Wedel (1999), "International Market Segmentation Based on Consumer Product Relations," *Journal of Marketing Research,* 36, No. 1, 1-17.

Taylor, William (1993), "Message and Muscle: An Interview with Swatch Titan Nicolas Hayek," *Harvard Business Review*, 71, 99-110.

Trout, Jack, and Steve Rivkin (1996), The New Positioning: The Latest on the World's #I, *Business Strategy,* New York: McGraw-Hill.

Vogel, R. H. (1976), "Uses of Managerial Perceptions in Clustering Countries," *Journal of Internationa Business Studies,* 91-100.

Wasilewski, Nikolai (1993), "Dimensions of Environmental Scanning Systems in Multinational Enterprises," Pace University, Working Papers No. 3.

Wolfe (1994), "Comparing U.S. and Japanese Market Research Firms." *California Management Review*, 36 (Summer): 49-69.

Wolfe, Bonnie Heineman (1991), "Finding the International Niche: A 'How to' for American Small Business," *Business Horizons*, 34, No. 2, 13-17.

Womack, James P., Daniel T. Jones, and Daniel Roos (1990), The Machine That Changed the World, New York: Harper-Collins.

Weigand, Robert E. (1991), "Parallel Import Channels Optics for Preserving Territorial Intetgrity," *Columbia Journal of World Business*, 26, No. 1 (Spring), 53-60.

Zavrl, Frani, and Dejan Vercic (1995), "Performing Public Relations in Central and Eastern Europe," *International Public Relations Journal*, 18, No. 2, 21-23.